Strategic Thinking

An AI's Guide to 100 Strategies for Long-Term Success Using Game Theory and Strategic Planning

Table of Contents

Introduction: A Blueprint for Strategic Mastery

Imagine standing on a chessboard where every piece represents a decision, every move ripples through the game, and every player has their own hidden agenda. This is life — an intricate dance of game plans, competition, and opportunity. While life doesn't come with a playbook, it does come with patterns, principles, and solutions that can be learned, mastered, and applied.

Who This Book Is For

This book is designed for anyone who aspires to think several steps ahead — whether you're a leader, entrepreneur, student, or someone navigating the complexities of life itself.

Each chapter delivers a clear, practical plan you can apply immediately. These systems are not just limited to winning in traditional "games" such as business or negotiations. They're equally valuable for personal growth, managing risks, fostering relationships, and navigating life's uncertainties. From mastering the timing of critical decisions to transforming failure into opportunity, you'll find tools here to help you achieve long-term success.

Why should you read this book?

Strategy isn't just for CEOs or chess masters. It's for anyone who wants to live deliberately. It's a mindset that equips you with the ability to anticipate challenges, plan your actions, and pivot effectively when circumstances change. It empowers you to see the bigger picture while keeping an eye on the details. In a world of noise, distractions, and constant competition, the ability to think tactically is your greatest advantage.

What You'll Gain

With this book you will:

- Gain insights from game theory, which will teach you to see decisions as part of a larger system where every action has a reaction.
- Learn how to uncover hidden opportunities in partnerships, neutralize opponents' advantages, and make calculated risks that pay off.
- Discover the power of adapting to change and using uncertainty as a tool rather than a threat.

It's time to think ahead, act wisely, and win confidently. Let's begin.

Part 1: Foundational Strategies

Strategic thinking begins with a strong foundation — a set of principles that guide your decisions and actions, regardless of the situation. This section lays the groundwork for effective strategy by teaching you how to think beyond the immediate, prioritize clarity, and harness the subtle dynamics of competition and collaboration. By mastering these concepts, you'll create a robust mental framework to support the more advanced strategies that follow.

Chapter 1: Play the Long Game, Not the Next Move

When faced with a decision, many people fall into the trap of thinking only about their immediate next step. However, life rewards those who can think ahead. To "play the long game" means to approach every decision with a focus on the bigger picture. It's about resisting the temptation of short-term gains and prioritizing actions that align with your long-term objectives.

In the world of strategy, short-sightedness can cost you dearly. Imagine a chess player so focused on capturing a pawn that they fail to notice their opponent setting up a checkmate. In life, this translates to chasing small wins — such as a quick sale, a flashy promotion, or instant gratification.

The long game requires patience, foresight, and a commitment to outcomes that may not pay off immediately. This doesn't mean ignoring short-term actions altogether. Rather, it's about ensuring that each step aligns with your overarching goals. Think of each decision as a domino. Knock it down in the right direction, and it triggers a cascade of events that lead to your desired outcome.

Why People Struggle with Long-Term Thinking

Many people default to short-term thinking because it feels tangible. Immediate results are easy to see, measure, and celebrate. Long-term goals, on the other hand, can feel distant, abstract, and uncertain. This uncertainty often discourages people from committing to the long game.

But here's the secret: short-term wins are often fleeting. They may feel satisfying in the moment, but they rarely contribute to lasting success. Long-term thinking, while harder to maintain, creates a framework for sustained growth and meaningful accomplishments.

How to Play the Long Game

1. **Clarify Your Big Picture Goals:** Start by identifying what you truly want to achieve. Whether it's financial independence, career fulfillment, or personal growth, write down your long-term vision in specific terms.

2. **Align Short-Term Actions with Long-Term Goals:** Before making any decision, ask yourself, "Does this move me closer to my ultimate goal?" If not, reconsider.

3. **Accept Delayed Gratification:** Long-term success often requires sacrifices in the short term. Practice saying no to distractions that don't serve your bigger purpose.

4. **Review and Adjust:** The long game isn't static. Periodically review your progress and adjust your actions to stay aligned with your vision.

Real-World Example

Take the story of Amazon. In its early days, Amazon's founder Jeff Bezos deliberately chose to prioritize long-term growth over immediate profits. Investors criticized the company's unprofitable model, but Bezos stuck to his strategy of reinvesting revenues into expansion. Today, Amazon dominates in the global market because it played the long game when others didn't.

Exercises

1. **Personal Assessment:** Think of a decision you've made recently. Was it focused on short-term results or long-term impact? Write down what you would do differently if you were playing the long game.

2. **Long-Term Mapping:** Choose a long-term goal in your life. Break it into smaller milestones that align with your overall vision. Write down one immediate action you can take to move closer to your first milestone.

3. **Practice Delayed Gratification:** Identify one habit or behavior that prioritizes short-term satisfaction (e.g. impulse spending, procrastination). Commit to replacing it with an action that supports your long-term goals for one week.

Key Takeaway

Short-term wins may feel gratifying, but they rarely lead to lasting success. When you play the long game, every move contributes to a broader vision, ensuring your efforts build momentum toward meaningful and lasting outcomes.

Chapter 2: Begin with the End in Mind

Most people start projects or make decisions with enthusiasm but little thought about where they're headed. It's like starting a road trip without knowing the destination. You may drive fast and far, but you could end up in the wrong place entirely. To truly succeed, you must *begin with the end in mind*.

This strategy is about defining your ultimate goal before taking the first step. When you're clear on your destination, every decision becomes easier because you can evaluate whether it moves you closer to or farther from your goal. Without this understanding, you risk wasting time, resources, and energy on actions that don't contribute to meaningful outcomes.

Why It Matters

Envisioning the end allows you to reverse-engineer success. Think of an architect designing a building. They don't start by laying bricks randomly; they begin with a blueprint that shows the completed structure. Similarly, knowing your "end" ensures that each action you take builds toward a coherent outcome.

This principle applies in every domain — personal, professional, or even interpersonal. Whether you're starting a business, planning a career, or improving a relationship, you need to define what success looks like to achieve it.

How to Apply This Strategy

1. **Define Success:** What does the "end" look like for you? Be specific. A vague goal like "be happy" isn't actionable. Instead, aim for "a career that balances creative fulfillment with financial stability."

2. **Work Backward:** Identify the key milestones that lead to your goal. Break the journey into smaller steps, ensuring each builds on the last.

3. **Stay Flexible:** The end goal can evolve over time, but the insights it provides keeps you focused, even as circumstances change.

Real-world Example

Consider Pixar, the animation studio known for its blockbuster films. When Pixar begins creating a movie, they don't start with character design or animation. They start with the story's ending — how the audience should feel as the credits roll. This focus on the end goal ensures that every element of the movie serves the overarching narrative, resulting in powerful storytelling.

Exercises

1. **Vision Statement:** Write a one-paragraph description of your ideal outcome for a current project, goal, or challenge. Be as specific as possible.

2. **Milestone Mapping:** Identify three key milestones that will help you move toward this outcome. For each milestone, write one action step you can take this week.

3. **Future Reflection:** Imagine yourself one year from now, having achieved your goal. Write a letter to your present self-describing what you did to succeed.

Key Takeaway

Starting with the end in mind creates a clear path to success, ensuring every action you take builds toward a meaningful and coherent outcome.

Chapter 3: Prioritize Clarity Over Speed

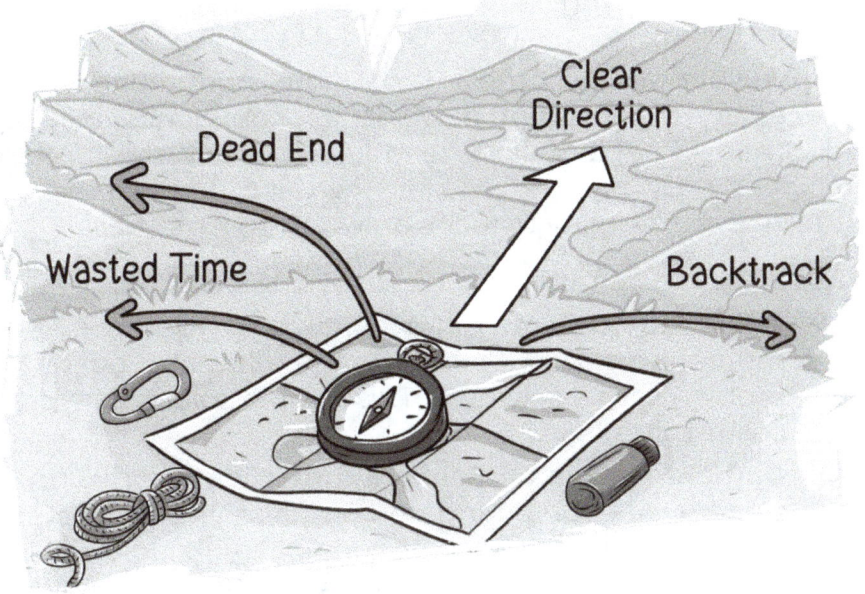

In today's fast-paced world, the pressure to act quickly is overwhelming. Everyone seems to value speed — fast results, instant decisions, and quick wins. But speed alone can be deceptive. Moving fast without understanding your direction is like sprinting into the fog — you might cover ground, but you could be heading straight for a cliff. Focusing on clarity instead of speed is the key to avoiding this common pitfall.

This strategy is not about procrastination or endless deliberation. It's about thinking before acting. Without focus, you risk missteps, wasted resources, and unnecessary stress — all of which slow you down in the long run.

Why Sharpness is a Superior Advantage

Clear thinking aligns your decisions with your larger goals and ensures your actions solve the right problem. Acting without vision often results in "busy work" — you feel productive, but nothing meaningful is accomplished.

For example, in business, teams often rush to implement solutions before fully diagnosing the issue. They might introduce new software to increase efficiency, only to discover later that the real problem was outdated workflows. This reactive approach creates additional problems that could have been avoided with a moment of pause and deeper understanding.

When certainty comes first, you not only eliminate unnecessary detours but also inspire confidence in yourself and others. People follow leaders who act decisively *and* intelligently. By pausing to gain certainty, you demonstrate wisdom and the ability to focus on what truly matters.

How to Prioritize Clarity Over Speed

1. **Pause to Reflect:** Before making a decision, take a moment to ask, "What is the ultimate goal? What problem am I solving?" This simple pause can prevent costly mistakes.

2. **Gather Context:** Seek information from multiple sources. Are you acting on complete and accurate data, or are you making assumptions?

3. **Focus on the Root Cause:** Don't rush to treat symptoms. Dig deeper to identify the underlying issue. For example, if your team is missing deadlines, is it due to poor time management, unclear instructions, or a deeper cultural issue?

4. **Communicate Effectively:** Misunderstandings often arise from unclear communication. Before moving forward, ensure everyone involved shares the same understanding of the goal and strategy.

Real-World Example

Consider the story of Toyota's legendary success. One of the cornerstones of Toyota's production system is the principle of "stopping to fix problems." When an issue arises on the production line, Toyota employees are trained to pause operations and thoroughly investigate the root cause before continuing. While this approach may seem counterproductive in the moment, it ultimately saves time, reduces waste, and improves quality.

Now, compare this to companies that rush to meet deadlines without addressing systemic issues. Their short-term speed often leads to product recalls, customer dissatisfaction, and long-term reputational damage. Toyota's commitment to precision has allowed it to maintain a reputation for reliability and excellence over decades.

Exercises

1. **Purpose Planner:** Identify a decision you're currently facing. Write down everything you know about the situation. Then, list any gaps in your understanding. What questions need to be answered before you proceed?

2. **Root Cause Analysis:** Choose a problem you're currently dealing with. Use the "5 Whys" technique—ask "why" five times to drill down to the root cause. Write down the true issue and potential solutions.

3. **Team Alignment:** If working with others, ask each team member to explain the goal of your project in their own words. Compare responses to uncover misalignments and clarify expectations.

Key Takeaway

Speed without direction leads to wasted effort. Clarity may take a little more time up front, but it prevents costly mistakes and ensures meaningful progress.

Chapter 4: Leverage Asymmetry in Resources

SMART USE OF RESOURCES

Big Goal

Many people assume that success requires having more money, more time, or more resources. However, history is filled with examples of individuals and organizations that achieved extraordinary results despite having fewer resources than their competitors. The key to their success? They leveraged asymmetry.

Asymmetry means recognizing the unique strengths you have — even if they seem small or unconventional. When you think strategically about your resources, you can outmaneuver competitors who rely solely on brute force or size.

Understanding Asymmetry

Asymmetry arises when two parties have unequal resources, skills, or abilities. While this might seem like a disadvantage, it often creates opportunities. Smaller players can act with agility and creativity, while larger ones may be constrained by bureaucracy or rigid systems. The key is to find ways to amplify the strengths you *do* have and use them in ways that your opponent cannot counter.

For example, in the business world, start-ups often lack the financial power of established corporations. Yet, they frequently succeed by using speed, innovation, and niche focus to carve out market dominance. They recognize that their small size allows them to take risks and adapt quickly, advantages that larger companies often lack.

How to Leverage Asymmetry

1. **Identify Your Unique Strengths:** Start by listing the resources, skills, or attributes you have that others might not. These could include specialized knowledge, agility, creativity, or the ability to take calculated risks.

2. **Think Creatively:** Use your strengths in unexpected ways. For example, if you lack funding, you might focus on building partnerships or offering a highly personalized experience that bigger competitors can't replicate.

3. **Exploit Weaknesses in Larger Systems:** Look for areas where bigger competitors are slow, inflexible, or overextended, and position yourself to fill the gaps they overlook.

4. **Focus on Precision:** Instead of spreading resources thin, concentrate them on a single, high-impact objective. A well-aimed slingshot can accomplish more than a scattered barrage.

Real-World Example

Consider the story of Airbnb. When it launched, the founders didn't have the resources to compete directly with the massive hotel industry. Instead, they identified an asymmetry: hotels were impersonal, expensive, and lacked variety. By leveraging this gap, Airbnb created a platform where homeowners could offer unique, affordable lodging options.

Despite its small beginnings, Airbnb's innovative use of technology and community resources allowed it to disrupt an entire industry.

Exercises

1. **Resource Audit:** Write down all the resources, skills, and strengths you currently have — even those that seem minor or unconventional. Next, identify one challenge or competitor you're facing. How can you use your unique strengths to gain an advantage?

2. **Spot the Weakness:** Identify a competitor, organization, or problem that seems overwhelming. What weaknesses or blind spots can you exploit to turn the situation to your advantage?

3. **Create a Focused Plan:** Choose one specific strength you have and outline a plan to use it in a high-impact way. This might involve targeting a niche audience, solving a specific problem, or creating a unique offering.

Key Takeaway

Success doesn't come from having the most resources. It comes from using what you have with precision and creativity. By leveraging asymmetry, you can turn even small strengths into powerful tools for achieving outsized results.

Chapter 5: Embrace Iterative Progress

Perfection is overrated. Waiting for an ideal moment often leads to missed opportunities. Success doesn't come from flawless execution on the first try — it comes from taking action, learning from the results, and refining your approach over time. This is the power of iterative progress.

Iteration means making continuous, small improvements instead of aiming for an all-or-nothing approach. By breaking your goals into manageable steps and focusing on improving incrementally, you create a system of steady growth. Each iteration builds on the last, propelling you closer to success while reducing the risk of catastrophic failure.

Why Iteration Matters

Think of iteration as a way to "fail forward." When you focus on iterative progress, every misstep becomes a lesson and every success becomes a foundation for the next step. This mindset not only makes daunting goals feel achievable but also increases your adaptability. In an unpredictable world, being able to adjust and improve as you go is far more valuable than rigidly sticking to a plan that doesn't work.

Consider the alternative: trying to achieve perfection in one go. This approach often leads to analysis paralysis, where the fear of making a mistake stops you from taking any action at all. Iteration, by contrast, embraces imperfection as part of the process.

How to Embrace Iterative Progress

1. **Break Down Big Goals:** Start by dividing your objective into smaller, actionable steps. Instead of aiming to "launch a successful business," focus on completing your first prototype or securing your first client.

2. **Act, Learn, Repeat:** After each step, evaluate the results. What worked? What didn't? Use this feedback to inform your next action.

3. **Focus on Consistency:** Iterative progress isn't about big leaps—it's about taking steady, consistent steps forward. Even small improvements compound over time.

4. **Stay Open to Change:** As you progress, be willing to adjust your approach. Iteration requires flexibility and a willingness to adapt based on what you learn.

Real-World Example

The story of Spotify's rise to dominance in the music industry is a masterclass in iterative progress. When Spotify launched, it wasn't the polished platform that users know today. Early versions were far from perfect but offered just enough value to attract users and generate feedback. By continually releasing updates, testing features, and refining its algorithms, Spotify grew into the global leader it is now.

Exercises

1. **Iterative Goal Setting:** Identify a big goal in your life. Break it into smaller steps and write down one action you can take today to move toward your first milestone.

2. **Evaluate and Adjust:** Choose a project you're currently working on. Assess your progress so far. What can you improve in your next iteration?

3. **Celebrate Small Wins:** Write down three small achievements from the past week that contributed to your larger goals. Reflect on how these incremental wins are moving you forward.

Key Takeaway

Progress isn't about perfection, It's about persistence. By embracing iterative progress, you create a system of continuous improvement, turning small, consistent actions into meaningful, long-term success.

Chapter 6: Balance Offensive and Defensive Moves

Every strategy involves a mix of offensive and defensive actions. Offense is about taking risks, seizing opportunities, and moving aggressively toward your goals. Defense, on the other hand, is about protecting your resources, mitigating risks, and securing your position. True strategic mastery lies in knowing when to attack and when to hold back.

Many people lean too heavily on one side. Some charge forward recklessly, exposing themselves to unnecessary risks, while others focus so much on safeguarding what they have that they miss opportunities for growth. To succeed, you must strike a balance between offense and defense, adjusting your approach based on the situation.

Why Harmony Matters

Imagine a sports team that plays entirely on offense, neglecting defense. They might score points quickly but will ultimately lose if they can't protect their lead. The same applies in life: without equilibrium, you risk overextending or stagnating.

Balancing offensive and defensive moves also builds resilience. Offense helps you grow, while defense ensures you can weather setbacks. Together, they create a stable foundation for long-term success.

How to Balance Offensive and Defensive Moves

1. **Assess the Situation:** Evaluate whether the current environment favors bold action or cautious protection. What are the risks and rewards?
2. **Set Priorities:** Define your primary goal—are you trying to gain ground or secure your position? Let this guide your actions.
3. **Stay Flexible:** The relationship between offense and defense isn't static. Be ready to shift gears as circumstances change.
4. **Monitor Resources:** Offensive moves require investment, while defensive moves preserve what you have. Always keep an eye on your resource levels.

Real-World Example

Early in its history, Netflix took an offensive approach by pioneering DVD rentals and later launching its streaming service. However, as competition grew, Netflix shifted to defense, investing heavily in original content to secure its market position. By balancing bold innovation with protective measures, Netflix has remained a dominant player in the entertainment industry.

Exercises

1. **Evaluate Your Current Status Quo:** Reflect on your current goals. Are you leaning too heavily on offense or defense? Write down one action to restore stability.
2. **Risk and Reward Analysis:** Identify one opportunity you're considering. List the potential risks and rewards. How can you mitigate the risks while maximizing the rewards?

3. **Shifting Gears:** Think of a recent situation where you were too defensive or too aggressive. What would you do differently to achieve a better footing?

Key Takeaway

Strategic success requires balancing bold, offensive moves with cautious, defensive ones. By adapting to the situation and managing resources wisely, you create a stable foundation for growth and resilience.

Chapter 7: Understand the Zero-Sum Game

Life is not always a win-win situation. In some scenarios, what one person gains, another must lose. These situations are called zero-sum games, where the total resources are fixed, and one party's victory is directly tied to another's defeat. Understanding when you're in a zero-sum game is crucial for making strategic decisions, as it requires a very different approach than situations where collaboration is possible.

What is a Zero-Sum Game?

In a zero-sum game, the sum of all outcomes is zero. If one person wins $100, the other loses $100. There's no room for mutual gain or shared success. Common examples include competitive sports, negotiations over a single asset, or battles for market share in a saturated industry.

Recognizing a zero-sum scenario allows you to focus your strategy accordingly. In these situations, collaboration is off the table, and your goal becomes maximizing your position while minimizing your opponent's. Misinterpreting a zero-sum game as a cooperative one can lead to costly mistakes, such as trusting an opponent who has no incentive to share the spoils.

Why It's Important to Recognize Zero-Sum Games

Not every competition is zero-sum. Many situations allow for shared growth, mutual benefits, or creative solutions that expand the "pie." However, when the stakes are truly zero-sum, any attempt at collaboration or compromise can weaken your position.

For example, if two companies are vying for the same exclusive government contract, only one can win. Collaboration isn't possible, and any concessions you make directly hurt your chances. On the other hand, treating a situation as zero-sum when it isn't can close off opportunities for cooperation and growth.

The key is to correctly identify the dynamics of the game you're playing. Is the pie fixed, or can it be expanded? Are you truly in competition, or is there room for a win-win outcome?

How to Succeed in Zero-Sum Games

1. **Prioritize Your Objectives:** Be clear about what you want and focus entirely on achieving it. In zero-sum games, distractions or concessions can cost you the win.

2. **Study Your Opponent:** In zero-sum scenarios, understanding your rival's strengths, weaknesses, and strategies is as important as knowing your own.

3. **Maximize Leverage:** Use every advantage at your disposal to strengthen your position. This might include controlling key resources, setting the terms of engagement, or using psychological tactics.

4. **Prepare for Trade-Offs:** Since every gain comes at the other's expense, be ready to negotiate strategically. Decide what you're willing to sacrifice to secure your most important goals.

Real-World Example

One of the most famous examples of a zero-sum game is the Cold War-era arms race between the United States and the Soviet Union. Both nations competed to amass nuclear weapons, knowing that any gain by one was perceived as a direct loss by the other. Collaboration wasn't possible in this high-stakes scenario, so both sides invested heavily in strategies that would tip the balance of power in their favor.

Exercises

1. **Identify a Zero-Sum Game:** Think of a situation in your life where resources or outcomes are limited (e.g. competing for a promotion). Write down the stakes and how your gain might directly impact others.

2. **Assess the Dynamics:** Reflect on a recent conflict or competition. Was it truly zero-sum, or was there room for mutual benefit? How might you approach it differently if it wasn't zero-sum?

3. **Plan Your Strategy:** For a zero-sum scenario you're currently facing, outline three actions you can take to maximize your chances of winning without unnecessary concessions.

Key Takeaway

Zero-sum games demand a clear, focused strategy where every gain or loss is directly tied to the outcome. Recognizing when you're in a zero-sum scenario ensures you avoid unnecessary compromises and position yourself for maximum success.

Chapter 8: Find Win-Win Opportunities

Not every situation has to be a competition. Many scenarios allow for collaboration, creativity, and shared success. The art of finding win-win opportunities lies in recognizing these situations and fostering outcomes that benefit all parties.

Understanding Win-Win Dynamics

A win-win situation occurs when cooperation creates mutual value. This often requires shifting from a competitive mindset to one focused on shared goals. In business, win-win deals might involve forming partnerships, combining strengths, or negotiating terms that satisfy both sides.

For example, imagine two businesses competing for customers in the same neighborhood. Instead of undercutting each other's prices, they could form a partnership to host a joint event, attracting more customers to both. This collaboration benefits both parties far more than direct competition.

How to Create Win-Win Outcomes

1. **Identify Shared Interests:** Look for common goals or values that both sides can work toward. What does the other party want that aligns with your objectives?

2. **Expand Opportunities:** Instead of fighting over limited resources, explore ways to create additional value. This might involve finding creative solutions or redefining the problem.

3. **Communicate Openly:** Building trust is essential for collaboration. Be transparent about your goals and encourage the other party to do the same.

4. **Stay Flexible:** Win-win outcomes often require compromise. Be willing to adjust your approach to find a solution that benefits everyone.

Real-World Example

Consider the relationship between Tesla and Panasonic. Tesla, as an electric vehicle manufacturer, relies on high-quality batteries, while Panasonic specializes in battery production. Instead of operating as competitors, the two companies formed a partnership to develop better batteries together. This collaboration expanded the market for both, creating mutual gains that wouldn't have been possible otherwise.

Exercises

1. **List Shared Goals:** Think of a current conflict or negotiation you're involved in. Write down what you want and what the other party might want. Are there areas where your goals overlap?

2. **Brainstorm Solutions:** For a challenge you're facing, list three creative ways to "expand the pie" and create additional value for all parties involved.

3. **Build Trust:** Identify one relationship or negotiation where trust is low. What steps can you take to build credibility and encourage collaboration?

Key Takeaway

Win-win opportunities allow both sides to achieve greater success than they could alone. By focusing on shared goals and creating mutual value, they can turn potential conflicts into powerful collaborations.

Chapter 9: Evaluate Trade-Offs in Every Decision

Every choice you make comes at a cost. Choosing one option means giving up something else — this is the essence of a trade-off. Strategic thinkers understand that decisions aren't about having everything but about making deliberate choices that maximize value. To make the best decisions, you must evaluate trade-offs carefully, weighing the potential benefits against the sacrifices required.

Trade-offs are everywhere, from personal decisions like how to spend your time to professional choices such as allocating limited resources. Do you focus on short-term gains or invest in long-term growth? Do you prioritize speed or quality? Understanding and analyzing these trade-offs is essential for navigating complexity and making sound strategic decisions.

Why Trade-Offs Matter

It's tempting to believe you can have it all, but reality doesn't work that way. Resources such as time, money, and energy are finite. When you commit to one path, you inherently close off others. By failing to acknowledge trade-offs, you risk spreading yourself too thin, making decisions impulsively, or pursuing conflicting goals.

Consider a company deciding between investing in product development or marketing. Product development may lead to better long-term growth, but without strong marketing, sales might suffer in the short term. There's no "right" answer — it depends on the company's priorities and situation.

How to Evaluate Trade-Offs Effectively

1. **Clarify Your Priorities:** Before making a decision, identify what matters most to you or your organization. Are you optimizing for speed, cost, quality, or something else?

2. **Identify the Opportunity Cost:** Opportunity cost is the value of what you give up by choosing one option over another. Ask yourself, "What am I sacrificing by saying yes to this?"

3. **Quantify the Costs and Benefits:** Assign tangible values to the pros and cons of each option. This can include time, money, effort, or impact.

4. **Consider the Long-Term Impact:** Don't just think about immediate gains. Ask how each option aligns with your long-term goals.

5. **Involve Stakeholders:** If the decision affects others, involve them in the process to ensure you're considering all perspectives.

Real-World Example

The legendary investor Warren Buffett often speaks about the importance of trade-offs. Buffett is known for declining numerous opportunities, even lucrative ones, because they don't align with his core investment philosophy. Rather than chasing high-risk, high-reward tech stocks during the dot-com boom, Buffett focused on steady, reliable investments. While he missed some short-term gains, his disciplined approach to evaluating trade-offs has made him one of the most successful investors in history.

Exercises

1. **Opportunity Cost Exercise:** Think about a recent decision you made. Write down what you chose and what you gave up by making that choice. Reflect on whether the trade-off was worth it.

2. **Prioritization Matrix:** For a current challenge, list all possible options and rank them based on their alignment with your goals, resources required, and potential benefits.

3. **Long-Term View:** Choose one decision you're facing right now. Write down the short-term and long-term impacts of each option. Which choice best supports your larger vision?

Key Takeaway

Every decision involves trade-offs, and success depends on recognizing and evaluating them wisely. By clarifying priorities, understanding opportunity costs, and focusing on long-term goals, you can make choices that maximize value and minimize regret.

Chapter 10: Don't Confuse Luck with Strategy

Success often has two ingredients: skill and luck. But humans are wired to see patterns, even where none exist, which leads them to overestimate how much control they have over outcomes.

This chapter is about recognizing the role of luck in your successes (and failures) and ensuring you don't mistake chance events for a brilliant strategy.

Why It's Dangerous to Confuse Luck with Strategy

When luck is mistaken for skill, it leads to overconfidence. A leader who attributes their success entirely to their strategic genius might double down on risky decisions, assuming they can replicate past results. Conversely, underestimating the role of luck in failures can lead to unnecessary self-doubt or abandoning a sound strategy.

Understanding the difference allows you to replicate what's within your control and account for what isn't. It also makes you more humble and adaptable — two qualities essential for long-term success.

How to Separate Luck from Strategy

1. **Evaluate Repeatability:** A good strategy produces consistent results, while luck is often unpredictable. If your success can't be replicated, chance likely played a role.

2. **Focus on Process, Not Outcomes:** A sound process doesn't guarantee success every time, but it increases your odds over the long run. Luck affects individual outcomes; strategy affects the overall trend.

3. **Identify External Factors:** Reflect on external conditions that may have influenced the outcome. Was timing a factor? Did you benefit from someone else's mistakes?

4. **Stay Humble:** Recognize that even the best strategies rely on some degree of luck. Humility helps you remain open to learning and improvement.

Real-World Example

Consider the career of athletes or actors who find early success. Those who attribute their success solely to talent often struggle when luck (like being in the right place at the right time) no longer favors them. However, those who combine skill with self-awareness build lasting careers.

Exercises

1. **Outcome Analysis:** Reflect on a recent success or failure. List all the factors that contributed to the result. Which ones were within your control, and which were due to external circumstances?

2. **Process Review:** Identify one key decision you made recently. Evaluate whether it was based on sound strategy or influenced by a lucky break.

3. **Luck vs. Skill Assessment:** Think of someone you admire. Reflect on how much of their success might be due to luck versus strategy. What can you learn from their approach?

Key Takeaway

Luck plays a role in every outcome, but long-term success depends on sound strategy. By focusing on processes you can control and staying humble about factors you can't, you'll make better decisions and improve over time.

Chapter 11: Cultivate Tactical Patience

Patience is often seen as passive—waiting for something to happen. But tactical patience is far from passive. It's a deliberate and strategic approach that involves resisting the urge to act prematurely, waiting for the right moment to strike, and using time as an asset rather than a limitation. This ability to wait for the most opportune moment is a hallmark of great strategists, from military leaders to business executives.

The Difference Between Patience and Tactical Patience

While ordinary patience involves enduring delays, tactical patience is about using time as a tool to improve outcomes. It requires focus, foresight, and the discipline to resist acting out of frustration or impulse. Tactical patience ensures that when you act, your timing and resources are aligned for maximum impact.

Think of tactical patience like waiting for the perfect wave while surfing. Rushing to catch the first wave you see may result in a short or chaotic ride. But waiting for the right wave gives you the momentum to glide further and more smoothly.

Why Tactical Patience Matters

Hasty decisions often lead to wasted effort, unnecessary risk, or missed opportunities. Tactical patience, on the other hand, allows you to:

- **Gather More Information:** Time can reveal hidden variables or additional details that improve decision-making.
- **Avoid Traps:** Acting too early might mean falling into a competitor's setup or a situation that wasn't fully prepared.
- **Maximize Resources:** Waiting allows you to align resources, whether it's finances, skills, or partnerships, for better outcomes.

At the same time, tactical patience isn't about endless delay. It's about balancing preparation with decisiveness — knowing when to act and when to wait.

How to Cultivate Tactical Patience

1. **Develop a Clear Goal:** Tactical patience is useless without a clear target. Know exactly what you're waiting for and why it matters.
2. **Monitor the Situation:** Regularly assess the conditions. Are they improving or deteriorating? Is the window of opportunity opening or closing?
3. **Prepare While You Wait:** Use the waiting period to strengthen your position. Train, gather resources, or refine your strategy so you're ready to act when the time comes.
4. **Resist Impulses:** When you feel the urge to act out of impatience or frustration, pause and ask, "Is this the best moment, or am I rushing?"
5. **Recognize the Right Moment:** Tactical patience doesn't mean waiting forever. Be ready to seize the moment when conditions align with your goal.

Real-World Example

The story of Apple's entry into the smartphone market is a prime example of tactical patience. By the early 2000s, mobile phones were already widespread, and competitors such as Nokia and Blackberry dominated the market. Apple could have rushed to release its own device, but instead, it waited. During this time, the company studied user behavior, refined its software, and developed the ground-breaking iPhone.

When Apple finally launched the iPhone in 2007, it wasn't the first smartphone, but it was the most refined. The company's tactical patience allowed it to disrupt the market with a product that redefined mobile technology, leaving its competitors scrambling to catch up.

Exercises

1. **Pause Before Acting:** Think of a decision you're currently facing. Write down why you feel the need to act now. Then, list three reasons why waiting might lead to a better outcome.

2. **Monitor and Adjust:** Identify a goal you've been working toward. Evaluate the current conditions—what signs would indicate it's time to act? Write these down.

3. **Preparation Period:** Choose a goal that requires timing. Use this week to prepare your resources, improve your skills, or refine your strategy while waiting for the right moment.

Key Takeaway

Tactical patience isn't about inaction; it's about timing. By waiting for the right moment to act, you maximize your impact, avoid unnecessary risks, and set yourself up for success.

Chapter 12: Harness the Power of Perception

Perception is a powerful tool in strategy. It shapes how others see you, how they respond to your actions, and even how you view yourself. The ability to influence perception can be the difference between success and failure. But harnessing perception isn't about manipulation or deception. It's about projecting the right image and ensuring your actions align with how you want to be seen.

Why Perception Matters

Perception often carries more weight than reality. In negotiations, people are more likely to trust a confident but prepared speaker than someone hesitant, even if both have the same information. In leadership, followers gravitate toward those who project calm and competence, especially in uncertain situations.

Strategists understand that people act based on what they believe, not necessarily what is true. By managing perception, you can guide decisions, build trust, and strengthen your position.

How to Harness Perception

1. **Define How You Want to Be Seen:** Decide what qualities you want to project — credibility, confidence, reliability — and ensure your actions reinforce them.

2. **Pay Attention to Body Language:** Non-verbal cues often speak louder than words. Stand tall, make eye contact, and speak clearly to convey confidence.

3. **Control the Narrative:** Be proactive in sharing your story. If you let others define you, their perception may work against you.

4. **Align Actions with Image:** Perception isn't about pretending. Ensure your behavior and decisions consistently reinforce the image you want to project.

5. **Understand Others' Perspectives:** Perception isn't one-size-fits-all. Tailor how you present yourself based on the beliefs, needs, and biases of your audience.

Real-World Example

Elon Musk is a master of shaping perception. While his companies (Tesla, SpaceX, and others) have faced significant challenges, Musk projects an image of visionary confidence. This perception has allowed him to attract investors, build customer loyalty, and maintain public trust even during setbacks.

However, perception must align with reality to be sustainable. Leaders who project confidence without substance often lose credibility once their promises fall through.

Exercises

1. **Self-Perception Audit:** Write down three words you think others would use to describe you. Compare them to the three words you want them to use. What actions can you take to bridge the gap?

2. **Body Language Practice:** For one week, focus on improving your body language. Maintain good posture, make consistent eye contact, and use deliberate gestures. Reflect on how others respond to you.

3. **Narrative Control:** Think of a situation where others misunderstood your intentions. Rewrite the story you want them to believe, and outline steps to communicate it more effectively in the future.

Key Takeaway

Perception shapes how others interact with you and how opportunities unfold. By managing how you're seen and aligning it with your actions, you build trust, credibility, and influence.

Chapter 13: Simplify Complex Options

When faced with too many choices, even the sharpest minds can become overwhelmed. This phenomenon, often called "decision paralysis," occurs when complexity hinders action. The solution? Simplify. This doesn't mean ignoring important details. It is about distilling complexity into actionable clarity.

Strategic thinkers excel at cutting through noise to focus on the core elements that matter. They understand that inaction often stems from an excess of options rather than a lack of them. Simplifying complex options allows you to see the bigger picture, make better decisions, and act with confidence.

Why Simplification is Crucial

Complexity is the enemy of efficiency. When too many variables are at play, the brain struggles to weigh pros and cons, creating delays or poor decisions. By reducing choices to their essentials, you free up mental energy to focus on execution rather than indecision.

Consider a business leader deciding where to allocate resources. A dozen competing priorities might feel equally urgent, but by focusing on the top two or three with the highest impact, the leader ensures progress without being bogged down by competing demands.

How to Simplify Complex Options

1. **Define Your Objective:** Start by asking, "What is the end goal?" This ensures that your efforts are directed toward what matters most.

2. **Group Similar Choices:** When options overlap, group them into categories. This reduces the mental load of considering each individually.

3. **Identify Key Criteria:** Choose two or three criteria that matter most to your decision. Evaluate each option based on these factors.

4. **Eliminate Low-Value Choices:** Discard options that don't significantly contribute to your goal. This narrows your focus to the highest-impact choices.

5. **Use Decision Frameworks:** Tools like decision trees or cost-benefit analyses can help organize complex information into a clear structure.

Real-World Example

Slack, the workplace communication platform, is a contemporary example of simplifying complexity to achieve success. When Slack launched, many companies were already using a mix of email, file-sharing services, and messaging apps to manage communication. Rather than trying to compete with each tool separately, Slack focused on simplifying workplace communication by consolidating these functions into one platform.

Exercises

1. **Pare Down Priorities:** List all the tasks or options you're currently considering for a project. Identify the top three that will have the greatest impact and focus on them.

2. **Create a Decision Tree:** For a complex decision you're facing, draw a decision tree to map out your options, their consequences, and how they align with your goals.

3. **Eliminate the Noise:** Reflect on an area of your life where complexity is holding you back. What unnecessary choices or distractions can you remove to create clarity?

Key Takeaway

Simplifying complex options isn't about ignoring details. It's about focusing on what truly matters. By cutting through the noise and prioritizing high-impact choices, you enable clear, confident decision-making that drives meaningful results.

Chapter 14: Always Ask "Why?" Twice

Curiosity is the foundation of strategic thinking, and asking "why?" is its simplest yet most powerful tool. But a single "why?" is rarely enough. The first answer often addresses symptoms rather than root causes. Asking "why?" twice — or more — forces you to dig deeper, uncovering the true dynamics behind a problem or opportunity.

This technique, known as the 5 Whys in problem-solving frameworks, is a hallmark of analytical thinking. By refusing to settle for surface-level answers, you gain a clearer understanding of situations, enabling more effective strategies.

Why Asking "Why?" Twice is Effective

Most people accept the first explanation they receive. While this saves time, it often leads to decisions based on incomplete or misleading information. By going deeper, you uncover the core issue, which is often more nuanced than it first appears.

For example, if a project misses its deadline, the immediate answer might be, "The team worked too slowly." But asking "why?" again might reveal that the real issue was unclear communication or insufficient planning. Tackling the deeper cause prevents repeat failures.

How to Use the "Why?" Technique

1. **Start with the Obvious:** Ask "why?" to address the most immediate or visible issue.

2. **Dig Deeper:** For every answer you receive, ask "why?" again. Repeat until you uncover a root cause or actionable insight.

3. **Avoid Assumptions:** Be cautious not to settle for assumptions or convenient answers. Challenge yourself to find evidence for each response.

4. **Focus on Solutions:** Once the root cause is clear, identify actions to address it directly, rather than just treating symptoms.

Real-World Example

In the early 2000s, Domino's Pizza faced declining sales and poor customer satisfaction. Initial surveys revealed that customers didn't like the pizza. But instead of stopping there, Domino's executives asked, **"Why don't customers like the pizza?"** The answer? It lacked freshness and flavor. **"Why does it lack freshness?"** Because the dough recipe and delivery methods hadn't been updated in decades.

This deeper questioning led Domino's to revamp its pizza recipe, improve its delivery processes, and launch a transparent marketing campaign that highlighted the changes. The result was a turnaround in both reputation and sales, proving that going beyond surface-level answers can lead to meaningful transformation.

Exercises

1. **Root Cause Analysis:** Think of a recent challenge you faced. Write down the first answer to "why?" and keep asking until you uncover the root cause.

2. **Challenge Assumptions:** Choose a belief or routine you follow without question. Ask "why?" twice to analyze whether it still serves you.

3. **Practice with Small Decisions:** Use this technique for everyday choices to build the habit of digging deeper into your reasoning.

Key Takeaway

By asking "why?" more than once, you move beyond surface-level answers to uncover root causes. This deeper understanding allows you to solve problems at their core and make more effective decisions.

Chapter 15: Avoid Overcommitting Help

Helping others is an essential part of building relationships and fostering trust. However, overcommitting your time, energy, or resources can backfire. When you stretch yourself too thin, you risk not delivering on your promises, burning out, or neglecting your own priorities. The key is learning how to offer meaningful help without overcommitting.

Many people fall into the trap of overcommitting because they fear disappointing others or believe saying "yes" to every request is the best way to build trust. While well-intentioned, this behavior can lead to missed deadlines, compromised quality, and a reputation for unreliability. Strategic thinkers understand that saying "no" is sometimes the best way to protect their ability to provide high-value assistance where it truly matters.

Why Avoiding Overcommitment is Important

Overcommitting doesn't just affect you. It also impacts those you're trying to help. If you take on too many requests, the quality of your assistance often suffers. By focusing your efforts, you ensure that the help you provide is effective and impactful.

How to Offer Help Without Overcommitting

1. **Assess Your Capacity:** Before agreeing to help, evaluate whether you have the time and resources to follow through without compromising other priorities.

2. **Prioritize Requests:** Not all requests are equally important. Focus on helping where your contribution will have the greatest impact.

3. **Set Boundaries:** Clearly communicate what you can and cannot offer. For example, agree to assist with specific tasks rather than taking on an entire project.

4. **Learn to Say "No" Gracefully:** Declining a request doesn't have to damage relationships. Be honest and suggest alternatives, such as other resources or people who may be able to help.

5. **Protect Your Own Priorities:** Helping others should never come at the cost of neglecting your personal or professional goals.

Real-World Example

Bill Gates famously faced challenges managing his time as Microsoft grew. Recognizing the risk of overcommitting, Gates adopted a deliberate approach to prioritize tasks and delegate effectively. By saying "no" to opportunities that didn't align with his long-term goals, he focused his energy on high-impact areas, such as developing ground-breaking software and growing Microsoft into a tech giant.

Exercises

1. **Track Your Commitments:** Write down all the tasks, favors, or responsibilities you've agreed to recently. Evaluate whether any of them can be delegated, delayed, or declined.

2. **Set a Help Limit:** For the next week, commit to helping no more than three people or projects. Focus on offering meaningful assistance to each.

3. **Practice Saying "No":** Reflect on a request you should have declined but didn't. Write a polite response you could use in a similar situation in the future.

Key Takeaway

Helping others is valuable, but overcommitting reduces the quality of your assistance and drains your resources. By focusing your help where it matters most and setting boundaries, you ensure that your efforts are both effective and sustainable.

Chapter 16: Be the First Mover When It Counts

In strategy, timing is everything. Being the first mover — someone who takes action before others — can provide significant advantages, such as establishing market dominance, shaping perceptions, or capturing key opportunities. However, being the first mover isn't always the best choice. The key lies in knowing when taking the lead will create lasting advantages and when waiting might be wiser.

Why First Movers Have an Edge

First movers often benefit from "first-mover advantage." This can include:

- **Brand Recognition:** Being first establishes your name as synonymous with the innovation or opportunity.
- **Market Share:** Early action allows you to secure resources, customers, or territory before competitors enter the field.

- **Shaping the Rules:** By moving first, you can influence how others view the market or opportunity, creating a standard others must follow.

However, moving first also carries risks. If the timing is wrong or the approach isn't well-thought-out, others can learn from your mistakes and gain an edge as "fast followers."

How to Decide When to Be the First Mover

1. **Assess the Landscape:** Is the opportunity time-sensitive, or could waiting allow for more preparation?
2. **Evaluate the Risks:** What are the potential downsides of moving first, and are you prepared to address them?
3. **Prepare Thoroughly:** First movers succeed when they combine speed with preparation. Moving first without being ready can lead to failure.
4. **Monitor Competitors:** If others are on the verge of acting, being the first mover may prevent them from gaining an edge.

Real-World Example

In the early 2000s, PayPal revolutionized online payments by being the first company to provide a seamless, secure method for transferring money electronically. At a time when e-commerce was gaining traction, PayPal's first-mover advantage allowed it to integrate quickly with platforms such as eBay. By establishing trust in the marketplace and becoming synonymous with online transactions, PayPal outpaced competitors and set the standard for digital payment systems. Its early action positioned it as a leader in the financial technology space.

Exercises

1. **Identify First-Mover Opportunities:** Look at your current goals or projects. Are there opportunities where acting first could provide a competitive advantage?
2. **Weigh the Risks:** For a decision where you're considering moving first, list the potential risks and benefits. How can you mitigate the risks?

3. **Plan Your First Move:** Choose one area where you can act decisively this week. Create a clear plan to ensure your first move is impactful.

Key Takeaway

Being the first mover can offer significant advantages, but only if the timing and preparation align. By acting decisively when it counts, you position yourself to shape outcomes and secure lasting success.

Chapter 17: Follow the Nash Equilibrium

In strategic decision-making, knowing when to compromise and when to hold your ground is critical. The Nash Equilibrium, a concept from game theory, provides a framework for understanding balance in competitive and cooperative situations. Named after mathematician John Nash, this principle occurs when all parties involved in a decision have chosen their best possible strategy, assuming the others won't change theirs.

The Nash Equilibrium is not about everyone winning — it's about reaching a state where no individual can improve their position without making someone else worse off. It's a critical concept for navigating scenarios where decisions are interdependent, like negotiations, market competition, or even interpersonal dynamics.

Why the Nash Equilibrium Matters

Many strategies fail because they assume that one party's actions are independent of the other's. In reality, most decisions are interconnected. By understanding the Nash Equilibrium, you can identify stable outcomes where neither side has an incentive to deviate.

Consider a price war between two businesses. If both undercut each other indefinitely, they'll erode their profits. Instead, by understanding each other's limits, they may settle at a price point that maximizes mutual benefit while discouraging further undercutting.

How to Apply the Nash Equilibrium in Real Life

1. **Analyze Interdependence:** Identify how your decisions affect others and how their actions impact you.

2. **Evaluate Stable Outcomes:** Look for strategies where no party has an incentive to unilaterally change their approach.

3. **Avoid Unnecessary Aggression:** Recognize when escalating a situation is counterproductive. Sometimes the best move is maintaining balance.

4. **Build Predictability:** In negotiations or partnerships, demonstrate consistency so others can rely on your strategy, leading to more stable outcomes.

Real-World Example

The global airline industry often operates around Nash Equilibrium principles. Airlines compete on ticket pricing, but unrestrained price wars would harm everyone. Instead, they often settle into pricing structures where each airline maintains profitability, knowing that aggressive under-pricing would trigger retaliation and mutual losses.

This equilibrium doesn't eliminate competition, but it ensures a balance where no single airline is incentivized to disrupt the market radically. Understanding this dynamic helps airlines remain competitive while avoiding destructive price wars.

Exercises

1. **Find a Nash Equilibrium:** Think of a negotiation or conflict you're involved in. What choices could create a stable outcome where neither party has an incentive to change their position?

2. **Assess Interconnected Decisions:** Choose a scenario where your decisions impact others. How do their likely responses shape your strategy?

3. **Simulate Stability:** Create a simple game with a friend, where both players make decisions that impact each other's outcomes. Look for the point where neither of you can improve without cooperation.

Key Takeaway

The Nash Equilibrium highlights the importance of interdependence in strategic thinking. By recognizing stable outcomes where no party benefits from unilaterally changing their strategy, you can navigate competition and collaboration with greater confidence.

Chapter 18: Build Redundancies for Resilience

In a perfect world, everything would go according to plan. But in reality, systems fail, people make mistakes, and unforeseen events occur. Building redundancies — backup systems, extra resources, or contingency plans — is essential for ensuring resilience. While redundancies may seem inefficient in the short term, they provide the safety and flexibility needed to thrive in uncertain environments.

Why Redundancies Are Crucial

Redundancies act as fail-safes. They ensure that when one system fails, another is ready to take its place. In business, this might mean having multiple suppliers for critical materials. In personal finances, it could involve an emergency savings fund. Redundancies don't just prevent failure — they allow you to recover faster and minimize disruption.

Space exploration is a good example. NASA incorporates redundancies into every mission, from backup communication systems to duplicate life-support mechanisms. These redundancies add weight and cost, but they're non-negotiable when the stakes are life and mission success.

How to Build Redundancies

1. **Identify Critical Systems:** Focus on areas where failure would have the greatest impact, such as finances, operations, or relationships.
2. **Create Backups:** Develop alternative resources, plans, or systems that can step in when the primary one fails.
3. **Test Your Redundancies:** A plan is only as good as its execution. Regularly test your backups to ensure they work under pressure.
4. **Balance Efficiency with Resilience:** Avoid excessive redundancy that wastes resources, but ensure you're prepared for high-stakes risks.

Real-World Example

The COVID-19 pandemic highlighted the importance of redundancies in global supply chains. Companies that relied on single suppliers for key components faced severe disruptions, while those with diversified suppliers weathered the crisis more effectively. This resilience through redundancy underscored the need for proactive planning in a volatile world.

Exercises

1. **Identify Vulnerabilities:** Write down three areas of your life or business where failure would have the greatest impact. What redundancies can you create to mitigate these risks?
2. **Create a Backup Plan:** For a project or goal, develop an alternative plan in case your primary approach fails.
3. **Test Your Systems:** Choose one critical area and test its backup. For example, try using an alternative supplier or accessing an emergency fund to ensure it works as intended.

Key Takeaway

Building redundancies ensures you're prepared for failures or unexpected events. By incorporating backups and contingency plans into critical areas, you create resilience and flexibility in the face of uncertainty.

Chapter 19: Don't Neglect the Cost of Inaction

The cost of inaction is often invisible but can be just as damaging as a bad decision. While most people focus on the risks of acting too quickly or making the wrong choice, they often overlook the hidden price of doing nothing. Strategic thinkers understand that inaction is rarely neutral. It usually results in missed opportunities, wasted potential, or worsening problems.

Inaction can occur for many reasons: fear of failure, overanalysis, or a desire for perfect conditions. But in most cases, waiting too long leads to greater risks than acting with imperfect information. The challenge is learning to assess when waiting adds value and when it merely delays progress.

Why Inaction is Risky

1. **Opportunities are Finite:** Many opportunities have a shelf life. Waiting too long can mean losing your chance to act altogether.

2. **Problems Escalate:** Unaddressed challenges often grow more complex and costly over time.

3. **Stagnation Stalls Growth:** Refusing to act keeps you in place while others move ahead, leaving you at a disadvantage.

Consider a business that hesitates to adopt new technology. While they deliberate, competitors who act early gain a technological edge, capturing market share and setting new standards. By the time the hesitant business decides to act, they're left playing catch-up.

How to Evaluate the Cost of Inaction

1. **Quantify Potential Losses:** Identify what's at stake if you choose not to act — missed revenue, declining market share, or personal growth.

2. **Compare Risks:** Assess whether the risks of inaction outweigh the risks of taking a calculated step forward.

3. **Set Deadlines:** Avoid indefinite delays by giving yourself a clear timeline to act.

4. **Start Small:** If you're unsure about a decision, take a low-stakes action to test the waters without fully committing.

Real-World Example

Kodak provides a cautionary tale of the cost of inaction. Although Kodak invented the first digital camera in 1975, the company hesitated to pursue digital photography for fear of cannibalizing its film business. While Kodak delayed, competitors such as Sony and Canon embraced digital technology, capturing the market and redefining the industry. By the time Kodak acted, it was too late. The company filed for bankruptcy in 2012, a victim of its own failure to adapt.

Exercises

1. **Identify an Opportunity:** Think of a decision you've been delaying. Write down what you stand to lose if you continue to wait.

2. **Risk Assessment:** Compare the risks of acting versus the risks of inaction. Which option has the higher long-term cost?

3. **Take One Step:** Choose a small, manageable action you can take today toward resolving a delayed decision.

Key Takeaway

Inaction has a cost, often greater than the risks of acting. By evaluating what's at stake and taking steps forward, you position yourself to seize opportunities and prevent problems from escalating.

Chapter 20: Master the Pivot Point

Even the most carefully crafted plans can hit obstacles, whether due to shifting circumstances, emerging competitors, or new opportunities. Success often hinges not on sticking rigidly to a failing course but on the ability to pivot — shifting your approach while maintaining focus on your ultimate goal. A well-timed pivot transforms challenges into opportunities, keeps your momentum intact, and positions you for long-term success.

A pivot can be as small as adjusting your tactics in a negotiation or as significant as completely redefining your business model. The key is to identify when a pivot is necessary and execute it with clarity and purpose.

Why Pivoting is Essential

1. **Adaptation Ensures Survival:** Markets, industries, and environments are constantly changing. Without adaptability, even the strongest strategies can become

obsolete. Pivoting allows you to adjust to these changes and remain competitive.

2. **It Protects Resources:** Continuing on a failing path wastes time, energy, and money. A strategic pivot redirects those resources to more promising opportunities.

3. **It Maximizes Learning:** Every obstacle provides valuable insights. Pivoting uses those lessons to refine your approach and make better decisions moving forward.

How to Pivot Effectively

1. **Clarify Your Core Goal:** Before pivoting, reaffirm what you're trying to achieve. A successful pivot shifts the approach without losing sight of the destination.

2. **Reassess Your Strengths:** Identify the resources, skills, or assets you already have that can support the new direction.

3. **Plan the Transition:** A pivot isn't a leap of faith. Develop a clear strategy for reallocating resources, setting new priorities, and communicating the change to stakeholders.

4. **Maintain Momentum:** A pivot isn't about starting over— it's about redirecting your existing efforts. Ensure continuity by leveraging what you've already built.

5. **Communicate Clearly:** If your pivot affects others— whether employees, customers, or partners—be transparent about why the change is happening and how it benefits the larger mission.

Real-World Example

Instagram's transformation into the platform it is today exemplifies the power of a strategic pivot. Initially, it was a location-based check-in app with several features, including photo sharing. However, users gravitated toward the photo-sharing function, while other features saw little engagement.

Recognizing this trend, the founders made a bold pivot: they stripped the app down to its core photo-sharing feature, rebranded it as Instagram, and focused on simplicity and usability. By pivoting at the right time, the team avoided spreading resources too thin and created a product that resonated deeply with its audience.

Exercises

1. **Evaluate a Current Path:** Identify a project or strategy that's underperforming. What signs suggest it may be time to pivot? Write down potential new directions.

2. **Redefine Your Goal:** Revisit your core objective for a long-term project. How might a pivot help you achieve it more effectively?

3. **Develop a Pivot Plan:** For a challenge you're facing, outline the steps needed to shift focus or strategy while maintaining continuity and momentum.

Key Takeaway

Pivoting isn't about giving up. It's about adapting to stay aligned with your goals. By recognizing when to pivot, planning your shift carefully, and communicating clearly, you turn obstacles into opportunities and maintain progress toward success.

Part 2: Competitive Strategies

In the game of strategy, competition is inevitable. Whether you're navigating business rivalries, political conflicts, or even personal challenges, success often depends on how well you handle opposition. This section dives into the art of competing strategically — leveraging your strengths, exploiting weaknesses, and staying one step ahead of your rivals.

Chapter 21: Make the Most of Your Competition's Blind Spots

Every competitor, no matter how skilled, has blind spots — areas they ignore, underestimate, or fail to notice. These blind spots aren't necessarily flaws in their strategy; they are often the natural result of human limitations, overconfidence, or an excessive focus on certain priorities. Your ability to identify and exploit these gaps can be the difference between an ordinary outcome and a decisive victory.

Blind spots come in many forms: overlooked markets, neglected risks, or assumptions that competitors take for granted. By honing your observational skills and strategically addressing these blind spots, you create opportunities that your rivals simply don't see coming.

Why Blind Spots Exist

Blind spots aren't just mistakes; they are often the by-product of focus. A business deeply committed to dominating one market may neglect emerging competitors in other areas.

A highly experienced leader might rely too heavily on old methods, failing to adapt to new trends. Blind spots can also arise from complacency, overconfidence, or cognitive biases that skew judgment.

Identifying and leveraging these blind spots gives you a competitive edge by capitalizing on areas where your opponent has made themselves vulnerable.

How to Identify Blind Spots

1. **Monitor Patterns:** Watch for areas where your competitor consistently invests their attention and resources. Blind spots often emerge in areas they neglect or deprioritize.

2. **Observe Their Assumptions:** Pay attention to what they assume about the market, their competitors, or their own strengths. Question whether those assumptions hold true.

3. **Listen to Feedback:** Customer complaints, industry trends, or even insider leaks can reveal areas where competitors are falling short.

4. **Analyze Resource Allocation:** Where are they putting most of their energy? Blind spots are often in the areas they've chosen not to focus on.

Real-World Example

When Southwest Airlines entered the market, it identified a significant blind spot in the airline industry: most competitors were focused on major hubs and long-haul flights, leaving short-distance travel underserved. Southwest capitalized on this gap by offering low-cost, high-frequency flights between smaller cities.

By prioritizing efficiency, quick turnarounds, and customer-friendly pricing, Southwest tapped into a market that traditional airlines had largely ignored. This strategic focus not only allowed the company to grow rapidly but also disrupted the airline industry, forcing competitors to adapt.

Exercises

1. **Competitor Audit:** Choose a competitor and list areas where they might be overinvested or underinvested. Identify one blind spot you could exploit.

2. **Test Their Awareness:** Introduce a small, unexpected action and observe their reaction. This can reveal how prepared they are to respond.

3. **Assess Your Own Blind Spots:** Reflect on areas of your strategy that you may be neglecting. Seek feedback from a trusted advisor to uncover weaknesses you might not see.

Key Takeaway

Your competitor's blind spots are your hidden opportunities. By identifying areas they overlook and acting strategically, you gain an edge that catches them off guard and puts you ahead.

Chapter 22: Focus on the Player, Not Just the Rules

When it comes to competition, most people focus exclusively on the rules of the game—the structure, tactics, and tools needed to succeed. While this is essential, it's equally critical to focus on the player. Competitors aren't machines; they're human beings influenced by emotions, biases, and individual tendencies. By understanding the person behind the strategy, you gain a powerful advantage.

Rules may create the framework for competition, but the player decides how to interpret and execute within those boundaries. Learning their habits, motivations, and vulnerabilities allows you to predict their actions, exploit their weaknesses, and adapt your approach to counter their moves.

Why Focusing on the Player Matters

Rules apply equally to everyone, but players approach them differently. A risk-averse competitor might avoid bold moves even when the rules encourage them. A highly confident rival might overreach, assuming their strategy is flawless. When you focus on the player, you see opportunities that the rules alone don't reveal.

Moreover, human behavior is often predictable. Patterns emerge over time — whether in decision-making, communication, or reactions under pressure. Understanding these patterns enables you to tailor your strategy to outsmart your opponent.

How to Focus on the Player

1. **Study Their History:** Review their past decisions and outcomes. Are there recurring themes in how they approach problems or challenges?

2. **Identify Their Triggers:** Observe what makes them confident, frustrated, or indecisive. Emotional responses often reveal underlying tendencies.

3. **Anticipate Reactions:** Based on their behavior, predict how they'll respond to specific actions. Use this knowledge to shape your strategy.

4. **Adapt to Their Style:** If they're aggressive, use patience to wear them down. If they're cautious, use bold moves to keep them on the defensive.

Real-World Example

In the 1972 World Chess Championship, Bobby Fischer used psychological tactics to gain an edge over Boris Spassky. Fischer didn't just play the game — he studied Spassky's habits, from his favored strategies to his reactions under pressure. By introducing unexpected moves and even subtle distractions, Fischer disrupted Spassky's focus and forced him to play reactively. This focus on the player, rather than just the game, helped Fischer secure a historic victory.

Exercises

1. **Opponent Analysis:** Choose a competitor and write down three patterns in their behavior. How could you use these patterns to anticipate their next move?

2. **Self-Reflection:** Identify one habit or tendency of yours that an opponent might exploit. How can you address it to avoid becoming predictable?

3. **Experiment with Reactions:** During your next competitive interaction, introduce an unexpected element and observe how the other party responds. Use this insight to refine your approach.

Key Takeaway

The game's rules may be fixed, but players interpret and act on them differently. By studying the person behind the strategy, you gain insight into their tendencies and can craft approaches that outmaneuver them effectively.

Chapter 23: Control the Tempo of Engagement

In any competitive scenario, controlling the tempo — the speed and rhythm of engagement — gives you the upper hand. Whether it's a negotiation, a business rivalry, or a debate, the party that dictates the pace often controls the outcome. By adjusting the tempo to suit your strengths and disrupt your opponent's, you can maintain momentum when it benefits you or slow things down to regain control.

Tempo management isn't just about acting quickly or slowly. It's about strategic pacing: accelerating when it forces your rival to make hasty mistakes or pausing to gather information, plan, or wear down your opponent's patience. The right tempo can destabilize even the most prepared competitors.

Why Tempo Control is Powerful

1. **Keeps You in the Driver's Seat:** Setting the tempo forces others to react to your moves instead of focusing on their strategy.

2. **Disrupts Opponents:** A slower tempo frustrates aggressive rivals, while a faster pace overwhelms cautious ones.

3. **Aligns Actions with Goals:** Controlling the tempo ensures you're moving at a pace that maximizes your strengths and minimizes your weaknesses.

For example, in negotiations, a fast tempo can create pressure for quick agreements, while slowing things down can give you time to gather more information and identify leverage points.

How to Control the Tempo

1. **Start with Observation:** Understand your opponent's natural rhythm. Are they fast-paced and impulsive, or methodical and slow?

2. **Set the Tone Early:** Begin interactions at your desired pace to establish control from the start.

3. **Vary the Tempo:** Use shifts in speed to surprise your opponent, keeping them off balance.

4. **Use Pauses Strategically:** Silence can be a powerful tool, forcing your rival to fill the gap and potentially reveal information or weaken their position.

5. **Stay Adaptable:** If your opponent tries to take control, adjust to regain the upper hand without losing sight of your objectives.

Real-World Example

Muhammad Ali's famous "rope-a-dope" strategy during his 1974 fight with George Foreman is a perfect illustration of tempo control. Ali deliberately slowed the pace by leaning against the ropes and letting Foreman exhaust himself with a barrage of punches. By conserving his energy and dictating the rhythm of the fight, Ali waited for the perfect moment to strike. In the eighth round, he unleashed a fast-paced counterattack, knocking out Foreman to win the match.

Exercises

1. **Identify Your Tempo:** Reflect on your natural pace in competitive situations. Are you fast-paced, methodical, or adaptable? How can you use this to your advantage?

2. **Practice Shifting Gears:** In your next discussion or negotiation, experiment with speeding up or slowing down the conversation. Observe how the other person reacts and adjust accordingly.

3. **Plan a Tempo Strategy:** Choose a current challenge or rivalry and outline when to accelerate and when to slow down to maintain control.

Key Takeaway

Controlling the tempo of engagement allows you to dictate the flow of competition, forcing opponents to play on your terms. By managing the rhythm strategically, you can destabilize rivals, maintain control, and align actions with your ultimate goals.

Chapter 24: Feign Weakness Where You Are Strong

Sometimes, the best way to exploit your strengths is to hide them. Feigning weakness in areas where you are strong can mislead your opponents into underestimating you, misallocating their resources, or exposing their vulnerabilities. This tactic allows you to maneuver with the element of surprise and strike when they least expect it.

Feigning weakness doesn't mean giving up your advantage—it's about appearing less capable while maintaining your true strength. This misdirection can create opportunities for decisive action when your rival is unprepared.

Why Feigning Weakness Works

1. **Encourages Overconfidence:** Rivals who perceive you as weak may become careless or complacent, leaving themselves vulnerable.

2. **Shifts Focus:** By downplaying your strengths, you redirect your opponent's attention to areas that don't matter as much.

3. **Creates Element of Surprise:** Opponents are less likely to prepare for a strong move when they perceive no threat.

For example, in a competitive bidding process, a company might initially appear disinterested to prevent rivals from driving up prices. When the time is right, they can step in with a strong offer and secure the deal.

How to Feign Weakness Effectively

1. **Understand Perception:** Assess how others view your strengths and weaknesses. Use this insight to shape their expectations.

2. **Downplay Capabilities:** Be subtle — don't overdo it. A convincing feint relies on appearing naturally weak rather than obviously deceptive.

3. **Time Your Move:** Wait until your opponent has fully committed to their assumptions before revealing your true strength.

4. **Avoid Becoming Predictable:** If you feign weakness too often, others may begin to suspect your intentions. Use this tactic sparingly for maximum impact.

Real-World Example

During the 1980s, Nintendo feigned disinterest in the home console market, allowing competitors like Atari and Sega to dominate early. Behind the scenes, Nintendo was perfecting its NES (Nintendo Entertainment System). By the time it launched, the NES was far more advanced than its rivals' offerings, quickly capturing the market. Nintendo's apparent lack of urgency lulled competitors into complacency, giving the company a decisive edge.

Exercises

1. **Analyze Your Strengths:** Identify an area where you excel. How could feigning weakness in this area create an opportunity to surprise your competitors?

2. **Create a Feint Strategy:** Outline a scenario where you could deliberately downplay your capabilities to mislead a rival or adversary.

3. **Evaluate Timing:** Reflect on a past situation where revealing strength too early backfired. How could you have timed your move better?

Key Takeaway

Feigning weakness where you are strong allows you to disarm opponents and catch them off guard. By using misdirection strategically, you gain the element of surprise and create opportunities to strike decisively.

Chapter 25: Cultivate Alliances to Outflank Threats

In the face of formidable competition or overwhelming challenges, alliances can be your greatest asset. By building strategic partnerships, you combine resources, knowledge, and influence to tackle threats from multiple angles. An alliance isn't just about teamwork—it's a calculated strategy to strengthen your position and neutralize competitors or obstacles.

Alliances can take many forms: formal partnerships, informal collaborations, or even temporary arrangements to address specific threats. The key is to align your interests with others in a way that benefits everyone involved. A strong alliance not only outflanks competitors but also protects you from becoming isolated in the heat of competition.

Why Alliances Are Powerful

1. **Shared Resources:** Alliances allow you to pool assets, such as expertise, funding, or infrastructure, to accomplish more than you could alone.
2. **Broader Reach:** Partnering with others expands your network, giving you access to markets, opportunities, or audiences that were previously out of reach.
3. **Divide and Conquer:** An alliance can enable you to divide responsibilities, allowing each partner to focus on their strengths.
4. **Neutralizing Rivals:** By aligning with others, you can collectively beat common threats.

For example, two small businesses in the same industry might form an alliance to negotiate better rates with suppliers or share marketing resources to compete against larger competitors.

How to Cultivate Effective Alliances

1. **Identify Common Goals:** Look for partners whose interests align with yours. A strong alliance depends on mutual benefit.
2. **Choose Complementary Strengths:** Seek allies who bring unique capabilities that fill gaps in your own strategy.
3. **Build Trust:** Alliances thrive on transparency and reliability. Invest time in building trust to ensure a lasting partnership.
4. **Communicate Clearly:** Define roles, responsibilities, and expectations from the outset to avoid misunderstandings.
5. **Stay Flexible:** Alliances are dynamic. Be prepared to adjust the terms or nature of the partnership as circumstances change.

Real-World Example

The strategic partnership between Starbucks and PepsiCo is a perfect example of using alliances to outflank threats. In the 1990s, Starbucks wanted to expand its presence in the bottled coffee market but lacked the distribution network to reach grocery stores and vending machines. PepsiCo, with its extensive distribution channels, faced increasing competition in the beverage market and sought new products to boost its portfolio.

The two companies formed an alliance, combining Starbucks' brand and coffee expertise with PepsiCo's distribution power. This partnership allowed Starbucks to dominate the ready-to-drink coffee market while helping PepsiCo diversify its offerings. Together, they outflanked competitors like Coca-Cola and Nestlé in the growing bottled coffee segment.

Exercises

1. **Map Your Network:** List potential allies in your field or industry. Identify how their strengths could complement your own to address a common challenge.

2. **Define Mutual Benefits:** Think of a current threat or obstacle. Outline how partnering with another person or organization could create a win-win solution.

3. **Build Trust:** Identify an existing partnership or relationship. Take one step this week to strengthen trust, such as sharing information or offering help.

Key Takeaway

Strategic alliances allow you to overcome threats and achieve goals that would be impossible alone. By combining strengths and aligning interests, you create a powerful force capable of tackling even the toughest challenges.

Chapter 26: Use Decoys to Distract and Mislead

Decoys are powerful tools in strategy. By presenting a distraction or false target, you misdirect your competitors' focus, causing them to waste time and resources on irrelevant pursuits. A well-placed decoy shifts attention away from your true intentions, allowing you to act decisively in areas your rivals aren't prepared for.

Using decoys effectively requires subtlety and timing. The goal isn't to deceive for the sake of deception—it's to guide your opponents' actions in a way that benefits your strategy. Whether in negotiations, competition, or warfare, decoys create opportunities to strike where it matters most while your rivals are preoccupied elsewhere.

Why Decoys Work

1. **Divert Resources:** Competitors focused on a decoy will allocate energy to the wrong areas, weakening their ability to counter your real moves.

2. **Create Uncertainty:** A convincing decoy makes it harder for rivals to predict your true intentions, forcing them to act reactively.

3. **Buy Time:** Distracting opponents gives you the breathing room to prepare, regroup, or execute your strategy.

For example, in chess, a player might sacrifice a lesser piece to distract their opponent while positioning their more powerful pieces for a decisive move.

How to Use Decoys Effectively

1. **Choose the Right Distraction:** A decoy should be credible enough to capture attention but expendable enough that losing it won't harm your position.

2. **Time It Perfectly:** Deploy your decoy at a moment when your opponent is most likely to react strongly.

3. **Control the Narrative:** Shape how the decoy is perceived to maximize its impact.

4. **Act Quickly:** Use the distraction to make your real move while your opponent is preoccupied.

Real-World Example

In the fast-food industry, Burger King has often used clever decoys to distract competitors and draw attention to its brand. One notable example was the "Whopper Detour" campaign in 2018. Burger King launched a promotion where customers could order a Whopper for just one cent — *but only if they were within 600 feet of a McDonald's location.*

The campaign created the illusion that Burger King was directing customers toward McDonald's, but the real goal was to distract McDonald's while driving attention and traffic to the Burger King app. The campaign was a huge success, resulting in over 1.5 million app downloads and strengthening Burger King's digital engagement. By using McDonald's locations as a decoy, Burger King successfully turned its rival's presence into an advantage.

Exercises

1. **Identify a Decoy Opportunity:** Think of a current competition or negotiation. What false target could you present to mislead your rival?

2. **Plan Your Real Move:** While your opponent is distracted, what action can you take to advance your true goal?

3. **Test Subtle Decoys:** In a low-stakes situation, introduce a small decoy and observe how others react. Refine your approach based on the results.

Key Takeaway

Decoys are a strategic way to mislead and distract your rivals, giving you the opportunity to act where it matters most. By directing their focus away from your true intentions, you gain the upper hand and create space for decisive action.

Chapter 27: Capture High Ground in Negotiations

In negotiations, securing the high ground gives you the ability to shape the conversation, frame the terms, and maintain leverage. The high ground isn't just about moral superiority — it's about positioning yourself so that the other party must negotiate on your terms. This could mean controlling key information, offering the most valuable resource, or influencing the timing and structure of the negotiation.

Capturing high ground requires preparation, insight into what the other party values, and the ability to establish authority without appearing inflexible. When done effectively, you can guide the negotiation toward a favorable outcome while maintaining collaboration and goodwill.

Why High Ground is Important in Negotiations

1. **Sets the Agenda:** The party in the strongest position often defines the rules of engagement, making it harder for others to shift the conversation.

2. **Increases Influence:** High ground allows you to frame your offer as indispensable or superior, making it difficult for others to challenge your terms.

3. **Minimizes Pressure:** With a strong position, you can negotiate with confidence, avoiding desperation or rushed decisions.

For example, if you have a unique skill set or exclusive resource, you're automatically in a stronger position to negotiate favorable terms. The other party needs what you offer, giving you leverage to secure better outcomes.

How to Capture High Ground

1. **Prepare Thoroughly:** Research what the other party values most. Position yourself as the provider of something they can't easily get elsewhere.

2. **Control Information Flow:** Share key details strategically while withholding information that could weaken your position.

3. **Define the Context:** Take the lead in framing the negotiation. For instance, if discussing pricing, emphasize value over cost to set the tone.

4. **Be the First Mover:** When appropriate, initiate the negotiation to establish your terms as the starting point.

5. **Stay Calm Under Pressure:** High ground is lost when you react emotionally or concede too quickly. Maintain composure to reinforce your position.

Real-World Example

In 1993, Nabisco negotiated the purchase of the SnackWell's brand from a smaller company. Nabisco used its high ground by highlighting its extensive distribution network and marketing capabilities, which the smaller company lacked. By framing the conversation around how Nabisco could elevate the brand's success — something the seller couldn't achieve on its own — Nabisco gained leverage to negotiate favorable acquisition terms.

By capturing the high ground early, Nabisco positioned itself as the solution, not just a buyer. This allowed them to close the deal while retaining control over the brand's future.

Exercises

1. **Assess Your Position:** Think of an upcoming negotiation or discussion. What unique value or advantage can you bring to the table to establish high ground?

2. **Frame the Narrative:** Write down how you'll present your position to emphasize your strengths and guide the conversation in your favor.

3. **Simulate a High-Ground Scenario:** Role-play a negotiation with a friend or colleague, practicing how to maintain control and reinforce your leverage.

Key Takeaway

Capturing the high ground in negotiations ensures you dictate the terms and maintain leverage. By preparing thoroughly, framing the conversation, and presenting unique value, you position yourself for success.

Chapter 28: Create False Choices to Frame the Narrative

In competition, the way a choice is framed often determines the outcome. By presenting false choices, you guide your opponent toward a decision that aligns with your goals, even if they believe they're making the choice independently. False choices aren't about deception — they're about shaping perceptions to create a sense of control while subtly influencing the decision in your favor.

For example, in a sales pitch, you might offer two pricing tiers: one high-value option and one less attractive, lower-value option. The customer feels they're making a choice, but both options benefit you. The real power lies in the framing, which steers them toward the outcome you've already prepared.

Why False Choices Are Effective

1. **Simplifies Complexity:** False choices reduce the number of options, making it easier for the decision-maker to choose without overthinking.

2. **Guides Decision-Making:** Framing the options subtly nudges the decision-maker toward the preferred outcome.

3. **Creates Illusion of Control:** People feel empowered when they believe they're making a choice, even if the options are designed to benefit you.

How to Create False Choices

1. **Define Your Desired Outcome:** Decide what result you want before presenting the choices.

2. **Design the Options Strategically:** Include at least one option that's clearly less desirable, ensuring the preferred choice stands out.

3. **Avoid Overcomplication:** Too many options can overwhelm the decision-maker. Keep the choices simple and focused.

4. **Anticipate Reactions:** Consider how your options will be perceived and adjust to ensure the framing aligns with your goals.

Real-World Example

In the fast-food industry, McDonald's often uses false choices in its menu design. For example, meal upgrades like "small, medium, or large" options create the illusion of choice, but the framing encourages customers to choose the medium or large size, which provides higher profit margins. By presenting these predefined options, McDonald's subtly guides customers toward decisions that align with its business goals.

Exercises

1. **Frame a Decision:** Think of a situation where you need to influence someone's choice. Write down two or three options that guide them toward your desired outcome.

2. **Practice Simplifying:** Take a complex scenario and reduce it to two clear choices. How can you frame these options to make your preferred outcome more appealing?

3. **Evaluate Past Choices:** Reflect on a time when you were presented with limited options. Did the framing influence your decision? How can you use this insight strategically?

Key Takeaway

Creating false choices allows you to shape the narrative and guide decisions subtly. By framing options strategically, you empower others to choose while ensuring the outcome aligns with your goals.

Chapter 29: Use a Divide-and-Conquer Approach

United Group   Divided Team

Divide and conquer is a timeless strategy that involves breaking a larger, unified opponent into smaller, more manageable parts. By isolating groups, teams, or resources, you weaken your rival's ability to coordinate and defend against your moves. This approach has been used in military campaigns, corporate rivalries, and political maneuvers throughout history.

At its core, divide and conquer works by creating divisions where there was once unity. These divisions may stem from exploiting differences in goals, creating distractions, or sowing mistrust. Once divided, your opponent's strength is diluted, and their vulnerabilities are easier to target.

Why Divide-and-Conquer Works

1. **Weakens Unity:** A divided opponent cannot act cohesively, making them easier to defeat or outmaneuver.

2. **Overwhelms Resources:** Isolated groups have fewer resources to resist your strategy.

3. **Creates Distrust:** Internal divisions reduce morale and increase inefficiency.

For example, in a corporate setting, divide and conquer might involve negotiating separately with departments that have conflicting priorities, weakening their collective bargaining power.

How to Apply Divide-and-Conquer

1. **Identify Fault Lines:** Look for areas where your opponent's unity is weakest, such as differing priorities or conflicting interests.

2. **Create Distractions:** Introduce competing goals or narratives that draw attention away from their shared focus.

3. **Isolate Key Players:** Target influential individuals or groups, reducing their ability to collaborate effectively.

4. **Exploit Internal Rivalries:** Encourage competition or disagreement within the opposing group to erode their cohesion.

5. **Act Decisively:** Once divisions appear, move quickly to capitalize on the weakened structure.

Real-World Example

The Roman Empire mastered the divide-and-conquer strategy in its military campaigns. When facing powerful coalitions of tribes or nations, Roman generals would negotiate peace with one group while attacking another, systematically dismantling alliances. By isolating their enemies and dealing with them individually, Rome was able to expand its influence and maintain control over vast territories.

This approach worked because it prevented unified resistance, allowing the Romans to defeat stronger opponents by dividing their resources and morale.

Exercises

1. **Identify Potential Divisions:** Analyze a current challenge or competitor. Where are their internal divisions or weak points in unity?

2. **Plan a Distraction:** Develop a strategy to introduce competing priorities or narratives that weaken your opponent's focus.

3. **Simulate the Approach:** Role-play a negotiation or conflict scenario where you use divide-and-conquer tactics to gain an advantage.

Key Takeaway

Divide and conquer allows you to weaken larger opponents by breaking their unity and isolating their strengths. By identifying divisions and acting strategically, you can defeat rivals and gain the upper hand.

Chapter 30: Benefit from the Overconfidence of Your Opponents

Overconfidence is one of the most exploitable weaknesses in competition. When rivals overestimate their abilities or underestimate yours, they become prone to missteps, risky decisions, and overextensions. By recognizing and capitalizing on this arrogance, you can turn their overconfidence into your advantage.

Overconfident competitors often act impulsively, take unnecessary risks, or neglect preparation. These behaviors create opportunities for you to strike decisively or position yourself more strategically. However, exploiting overconfidence requires patience, observation, and a readiness to act when the moment is right.

Why Overconfidence is a Weakness

1. **Leads to Mistakes:** Overconfident rivals often skip due diligence, leaving themselves vulnerable to errors.
2. **Creates Blind Spots:** They may ignore warning signs or dismiss potential threats.
3. **Encourages Overextension:** Overconfident players may stretch themselves too thin, leaving critical areas unprotected.

For instance, in a sales scenario, an overconfident competitor might offer aggressive discounts to secure a deal, only to damage their long-term profitability. By staying composed and highlighting your strengths, you can secure the client with a more balanced offer.

How to Exploit Overconfidence

1. **Observe Their Patterns:** Identify behaviors that indicate overconfidence, such as dismissive remarks or overly ambitious goals.
2. **Encourage Overreach:** Subtly validate their confidence, nudging them toward bolder, riskier actions.
3. **Stay Prepared:** Overconfidence doesn't mean incompetence. Be ready to act quickly if they falter.
4. **Focus on Your Strengths:** Use their dismissiveness as an opportunity to build quietly in areas they're neglecting.

Real-World Example

In the late 1990s, Nokia dominated the mobile phone industry and became overconfident in its market position. The company dismissed the emerging smartphone trend, believing its existing models were untouchable. Meanwhile, others capitalized on this arrogance by investing heavily in smartphone technology.

When the iPhone launched in 2007, Nokia's overconfidence left it unprepared for the shift in consumer demand. Within a few years, the company lost its market leadership. This downfall highlights how overconfidence can blind even the strongest competitors to disruptive threats.

Exercises

1. **Spot Overconfidence:** Identify a competitor or colleague who exhibits overconfidence. How does their arrogance create opportunities for you?

2. **Plan a Response:** Develop a strategy to exploit an overconfident rival's blind spots or overextensions.

3. **Reflect on Your Own Confidence:** Are there areas where you might be overconfident? How can you stay grounded and vigilant?

Key Takeaway

Overconfidence creates opportunities for exploitation by leading rivals to overlook risks or underestimate you. By observing their weaknesses and staying prepared, you can turn their arrogance into a decisive advantage.

Chapter 31: Pre-empt Competitors Through Purposeful Partnerships

Sometimes the best way to outwit competitors is not by direct confrontation but by forming alliances that cut them off from critical opportunities. Purposeful partnerships — deliberately crafted to strengthen your position — can pre-empt competitors by locking in resources, creating exclusivity, or establishing a dominant market position.

Pre-emptive partnerships are about thinking ahead. By aligning with key players, you secure advantages that make it harder for your rivals to gain a foothold. These partnerships can include exclusive supplier agreements, joint ventures, or collaborative projects that corner a market or secure a unique advantage.

Why Purposeful Partnerships Work

1. **Control Critical Resources:** Partnerships can give you priority access to supplies, expertise, or markets, leaving competitors scrambling to find alternatives.

2. **Enhance Credibility:** Partnering with respected players can increase your influence and reputation, making it harder for rivals to compete.

3. **Create Barriers:** Strategic partnerships can establish exclusivity, locking competitors out of valuable opportunities.

For example, by forming an exclusive partnership with a leading distributor, a company can dominate a market segment while competitors struggle to reach the same audience.

How to Form Purposeful Partnerships

1. **Identify Key Players:** Look for partners who have resources, networks, or expertise that complement your goals.

2. **Align Incentives:** Ensure the partnership benefits both parties to create a strong, lasting alliance.

3. **Move Early:** Partnerships are most effective when formed before competitors recognize the opportunity.

4. **Negotiate Exclusivity:** Whenever possible, secure terms that give you unique access to the partner's resources or capabilities.

5. **Communicate the Advantage:** Use the partnership to showcase your strengthened position, discouraging competitors from challenging you.

Real-World Example

In the 1980s, Intel and IBM formed a strategic partnership that transformed the computer industry. By aligning with IBM, Intel became the exclusive supplier of microprocessors for IBM's personal computers. This partnership not only propelled Intel to market dominance but also made it difficult for competitors to gain traction in the rapidly growing PC market.

The exclusivity of the Intel-IBM relationship pre-empted rivals from establishing similar deals, securing Intel's position as a leader in the tech industry for decades.

Exercises

1. **Identify Potential Partners:** List organizations or individuals whose resources or expertise align with your goals. How could a partnership with them strengthen your position?

2. **Create a Partnership Plan:** Choose one potential partner and outline the mutual benefits of collaborating with them.

3. **Evaluate Competitors:** Analyze how your competitors could benefit from similar partnerships. How can you act first to secure the advantage?

Key Takeaway

Purposeful partnerships allow you to secure resources, credibility, and influence that pre-empt competitors from gaining ground. By forming alliances strategically, you strengthen your position and create lasting barriers to entry.

Chapter 32: Set Traps by Shaping Expectations

In competitive strategy, shaping expectations is a powerful way to influence your opponent's actions. By creating scenarios that seem safe or appealing, you can guide rivals into traps—positions where their predictable choices give you a decisive advantage.

Traps are not about deception for its own sake; they are about leveraging human psychology and your rival's assumptions. By carefully shaping their expectations, you make their moves easier to anticipate and counter, putting them at a disadvantage before they even act.

Why Traps Work

1. **Exploit Predictability:** Competitors often act based on assumptions. Shaping those assumptions lets you anticipate their next move.

2. **Force Poor Choices:** A well-set trap limits your rival's options, guiding them into a position of weakness.

3. **Maintain Control:** By dictating the terms of engagement, you stay one step ahead while your opponent reacts to your lead.

For example, in business, a company might announce a lower-priced product line to distract competitors, prompting them to overinvest in countering the new threat while neglecting their core offerings.

How to Set Effective Traps

1. **Understand Your Rival's Assumptions:** Study their behavior and beliefs to identify how they're likely to respond.

2. **Create False Signals:** Present scenarios that appear to confirm their assumptions, leading them into predictable actions.

3. **Limit Their Options:** Design the trap so that your rival's choices are narrowed to those that benefit you.

4. **Strike at the Right Moment:** Once your rival falls into the trap, act decisively to capitalize on their weakened position.

Real-World Example

During the Battle of Austerlitz in 1805, Napoleon Bonaparte used a classic trap by deliberately weakening his right flank, creating the illusion of vulnerability. The opposing Allied forces, confident in their assessment, attacked the "weak" flank. However, Napoleon had anticipated this move and concentrated his forces elsewhere, cutting off and defeating the Allies decisively.

By shaping the enemy's expectations, Napoleon turned their predictability into his greatest advantage, solidifying his reputation as a brilliant tactician.

Exercises

1. **Analyze a Rival's Patterns:** Identify a competitor's predictable behaviors. How could you shape their expectations to guide their actions?

2. **Design a Trap:** Outline a scenario where you could create a false signal or opportunity to lure a rival into a position of weakness.

3. **Evaluate Your Vulnerabilities:** Reflect on areas where you might be falling into traps set by others. How can you stay vigilant and adapt?

Key Takeaway

Setting traps by shaping expectations allows you to control your rival's actions and turn their predictability into your advantage. By influencing their decisions, you create opportunities to strike decisively and secure victory.

Chapter 33: Win Battles, Avoid Wars

In competition, not every battle is worth fighting. Winning small, strategic engagements can often achieve your goals more effectively than engaging in drawn-out conflicts. Wars — whether in business, politics, or life — are costly, unpredictable, and often leave both sides worse off. By focusing on winning key battles while avoiding unnecessary wars, you conserve resources, maintain relationships, and position yourself for long-term success.

This principle is about being selective. Instead of aiming for total domination, prioritize battles that bring the greatest rewards with the least cost. This approach not only preserves your resources but also ensures that your victories are meaningful and sustainable.

Why Avoiding Wars Matters

1. **Minimizes Risk:** Full-scale conflict often leads to collateral damage, wasted resources, and unintended consequences.
2. **Preserves Relationships:** Battles can be resolved without burning bridges, keeping opportunities for future collaboration open.
3. **Maintains Focus:** Engaging in too many conflicts spreads your energy thin, weakening your ability to win where it matters most.

For example, in negotiations, it's often better to concede minor points to achieve your main objective. By avoiding unnecessary contention, you ensure the outcome aligns with your goals while keeping the process smooth and productive.

How to Win Battles While Avoiding Wars

1. **Identify Key Objectives:** Before engaging, determine whether the battle aligns with your long-term goals.
2. **Pick Your Fights:** Focus only on conflicts where victory will provide significant advantages.
3. **Avoid Escalation:** Stay calm and avoid retaliating unnecessarily, even if provoked. Respond strategically, not emotionally.
4. **Negotiate Where Possible:** Resolve smaller disputes diplomatically to conserve resources for larger challenges.
5. **Know When to Walk Away:** Sometimes, the best way to win is to avoid fighting altogether.

Real-World Example

In the tech industry, Microsoft demonstrated this strategy in its competition with Google over cloud services. Rather than engaging directly in a "cloud war," Microsoft focused on targeted battles, such as building Azure's strengths in enterprise solutions and hybrid cloud systems. This allowed Microsoft to carve out a dominant position in its niche without directly confronting Google's established dominance in consumer cloud services.

By strategically choosing its battles, Microsoft avoided unnecessary conflict and grew Azure into one of the world's leading cloud platforms, achieving its goals without wasting resources on unwinnable wars.

Exercises

1. **Evaluate Current Conflicts:** List the battles you're currently fighting. Which ones are aligned with your long-term goals, and which could you avoid?
2. **Prioritize Your Efforts:** Choose one conflict that offers the greatest reward and focus your energy there.
3. **Reflect on a Past Conflict:** Identify a time when engaging in a "war" led to unnecessary costs. How could you have resolved it more strategically?

Key Takeaway

Winning battles without engaging in wars allows you to achieve focused victories while conserving resources and avoiding unnecessary risks. By choosing your fights wisely, you position yourself for sustainable success.

Chapter 34: Undermine Rivals with Incremental Disruption

Not every victory requires a dramatic or sudden move. Incremental disruption—making small, consistent changes that undermine your rival's position—can be just as effective as a bold strategy. These disruptions weaken your competitors gradually, allowing you to gain ground while avoiding direct confrontation.

Incremental disruption is about patience and persistence. Instead of seeking immediate results, focus on steady progress that erodes your rival's advantages over time. This approach is less risky than a head-on challenge and often goes unnoticed until it's too late to counter.

Why Incremental Disruption is Effective

1. **Avoids Detection:** Small changes are harder to notice and respond to, giving you a stealthy advantage.

2. **Builds Momentum:** Incremental progress creates compounding benefits, leading to significant results over time.

3. **Preserves Resources:** Gradual disruption requires fewer resources than large-scale moves, making it more sustainable.

For example, in retail, a smaller competitor might gradually expand its product offerings to match those of a larger rival. Each addition chips away at the larger competitor's market share without provoking a full-scale response.

How to Undermine Rivals Incrementally

1. **Target Small Vulnerabilities:** Look for areas where your rival is slightly weak and make steady improvements there.

2. **Stay Consistent:** Commit to a long-term strategy of gradual progress rather than seeking immediate gains.

3. **Adapt Over Time:** Use feedback from each move to refine your approach and keep your rival off balance.

4. **Monitor Your Impact:** Track how your disruptions affect your rival's position and adjust accordingly.

Real-World Example

IKEA's approach to disrupting the furniture industry is an excellent example of incremental change. Instead of directly challenging traditional furniture retailers with luxury products or high-end showrooms, IKEA focused on small innovations that made furniture more affordable and accessible.

It introduced flat-pack furniture to reduce shipping and storage costs, developed self-service warehouses to streamline operations, and implemented in-store childcare to enhance the shopping experience. These gradual, customer-focused changes chipped away at traditional furniture stores' market dominance over time, positioning IKEA as a global leader in affordable, functional furniture.

Exercises

1. **Identify a Small Target:** Choose one area where you could make small, consistent improvements to challenge a rival's position.

2. **Develop a Plan:** Outline a step-by-step strategy for gradually increasing your influence or weakening your competitor's advantage.

3. **Track Your Progress:** Measure the impact of your incremental changes over time and adjust your approach as needed.

Key Takeaway

Incremental disruption is a patient, strategic way to undermine competitors and gain ground. By focusing on small, consistent improvements, you can achieve significant results while avoiding direct confrontation.

Chapter 35: Neutralize Emerging Risks Before They Escalate

In competitive strategy, emerging risks are like sparks. They may seem harmless at first but can quickly ignite into destructive forces if left unchecked. Success depends on identifying and neutralizing these risks early, before they escalate into major threats. This proactive approach ensures that your resources are focused on growth and opportunity, not damage control.

Emerging risks can take many forms: a new competitor entering your market, a subtle shift in customer preferences, or early warning signs of financial strain. While it's easy to dismiss these as minor concerns, strategic thinkers understand that ignoring them often leads to costly consequences later. Addressing these risks early allows you to maintain control and stay ahead.

Why Neutralizing Risks Early Matters

1. **Prevents Escalation:** Small risks are easier and less expensive to resolve than large crises.
2. **Maintains Momentum:** Addressing issues early minimizes disruptions to your goals and operations.
3. **Builds Resilience:** A proactive approach strengthens your ability to adapt and handle future challenges.

For example, a business noticing a slight drop in customer satisfaction can act immediately by gathering feedback and implementing improvements, preventing a larger exodus of customers later.

How to Neutralize Emerging Risks

1. **Identify Warning Signs:** Stay alert to small changes in your environment, such as market trends, competitor behavior, or internal performance metrics.
2. **Evaluate Impact:** Assess whether the risk has the potential to escalate and disrupt your goals.
3. **Act Decisively:** Once a risk is identified, take swift and focused action to address it.
4. **Monitor Continuously:** Keep track of resolved risks to ensure they don't re-emerge or evolve into new challenges.

Real-World Example

In the early 2010s, Netflix faced an emerging risk as customer preferences shifted toward more original content rather than licensing existing shows. Recognizing this trend early, Netflix began investing heavily in producing its own original series, such as *House of Cards* and *Stranger Things*.

By acting quickly to address this emerging risk, Netflix not only retained its subscriber base but also positioned itself as a leader in original programming. This proactive move helped Netflix outpace competitors like Hulu and Amazon Prime Video, who were slower to adapt to the same trend.

Exercises

1. **Risk Assessment:** Identify one small risk in your current environment. Write down its potential impact and a quick plan to neutralize it.

2. **Develop a Warning System:** Create a system to monitor early indicators of risk, such as regular performance reviews or customer feedback loops.

3. **Evaluate a Past Risk:** Reflect on a situation where a small problem escalated because it wasn't addressed early. What could you have done differently?

Key Takeaway

Neutralizing emerging risks before they escalate is key to staying ahead in any competitive scenario. By acting proactively and decisively, you prevent small issues from becoming major obstacles and ensure long-term stability and success.

Chapter 36: Channel Psychological Momentum

Momentum isn't just about progress. It's a psychological force that can influence how competitors, allies, and even yourself perceive a situation. When you have momentum, everything feels easier. Wins build on wins, confidence grows, and those around you are inspired to support your efforts. Channeling psychological momentum is a powerful way to maintain an advantage and sustain long-term success.

Momentum creates a sense of inevitability. When people believe you're winning, they're more likely to join your side or hesitate to challenge you. However, losing momentum can lead to self-doubt, erode morale, and embolden competitors. The key is to recognize when you have momentum and take deliberate steps to build and sustain it.

Why Momentum Matters

1. **Amplifies Success:** Small victories build confidence and create a domino effect, leading to larger achievements.

2. **Discourages Opponents:** Competitors facing a rival with strong momentum often hesitate or make mistakes under pressure.
3. **Attracts Support:** Momentum inspires others to align with you, whether they're customers, investors, or team members.

For example, in sports, a team on a winning streak often intimidates opponents and rallies fans, creating an atmosphere that reinforces their success.

How to Channel Psychological Momentum

1. **Celebrate Small Wins:** Acknowledge and share every victory, no matter how small, to build a sense of progress.
2. **Maintain Focus:** Momentum is lost when focus wavers. Stay aligned with your goals to keep the energy moving forward.
3. **Capitalize on Success:** Use momentum as a springboard to tackle bigger challenges or pursue new opportunities.
4. **Avoid Overconfidence:** Stay grounded and prepared to handle setbacks, ensuring momentum isn't derailed by complacency.

Real-World Example

In the 2020s, Zoom became a global household name seemingly overnight. While the COVID-19 pandemic created demand for video conferencing, Zoom's ability to channel psychological momentum set it apart from competitors like Microsoft Teams and Google Meet.

As millions of new users flocked to Zoom, the company celebrated milestones such as crossing 300 million daily meeting participants and releasing regular updates to enhance user experience. This momentum created a ripple effect, attracting more businesses, schools, and individuals to adopt the platform. By sustaining excitement through rapid growth and strong customer engagement, Zoom maintained its leading position even as larger competitors scrambled to catch up.

Exercises

1. **Identify a Small Win:** Write down one recent achievement and consider how you can use it to build momentum in your current goals.

2. **Plan a Momentum Boost:** Choose an area where you're progressing and identify one action to amplify that success.

3. **Reflect on Past Momentum:** Think of a time when you had strong momentum. What contributed to it, and how can you replicate those conditions?

Key Takeaway

Momentum is a compounding force that builds confidence, attracts support, and intimidates rivals. By channeling and sustaining psychological momentum, you create an unstoppable drive toward your goals.

Chapter 37: Adopt an Inside-Out Mindset

Great strategies often begin from within. An inside-out mindset emphasizes leveraging internal strengths, values, and capabilities to drive success, rather than reacting to external pressures. By focusing on what you can control — your resources, processes, and team — you build a solid foundation that withstands external challenges and creates sustainable growth.

Many competitors fall into the trap of chasing trends or mimicking rivals, but an inside-out mindset allows you to maintain authenticity, focus, and adaptability. When your internal framework is strong, you naturally project confidence and competence outward, influencing how others perceive and respond to you.

Why an Inside-Out Mindset Works

1. **Builds Resilience:** When external conditions shift, a strong internal foundation helps you adapt without losing direction.

2. **Inspires Confidence:** Clarity about your strengths and purpose creates trust among team members, customers, and stakeholders.

3. **Encourages Innovation:** Focusing on internal assets leads to unique solutions that set you apart from competitors.

For example, a company facing stiff competition might focus inward to streamline operations, refine its product offerings, or enhance its team's skills. These internal improvements create a ripple effect, strengthening its external market position.

How to Adopt an Inside-Out Mindset

1. **Assess Your Strengths:** Conduct a thorough evaluation of your core assets, skills, and resources.

2. **Define Your Values:** Ensure your strategies align with your mission and purpose, creating consistency and authenticity.

3. **Strengthen Core Capabilities:** Focus on improving areas where you already excel to gain a competitive edge.

4. **Avoid External Noise:** While staying informed about external trends is important, avoid reacting impulsively to competitors' moves.

5. **Measure Internal Progress:** Use metrics that reflect your internal growth, such as team efficiency or customer satisfaction, to gauge success.

Real-World Example

Nike's "inside-out" approach during its growth into a global brand is a perfect example. Instead of focusing solely on competing with other athletic brands, Nike concentrated on its core strengths: innovation in product design, understanding its audience, and creating a strong brand identity.

Nike's investments in advanced shoe technology, collaborations with top athletes, and its commitment to empowering athletes globally helped it differentiate itself. This focus on internal excellence allowed Nike to lead the market, even as competitors such as Adidas and Under Armour pursued different tactics.

Exercises

1. **Identify Your Core Strength:** Write down one area where you or your organization excels. How can you maximize this strength to improve your external results?

2. **Refine Internal Processes:** Choose one internal system or process that needs improvement. Create a plan to optimize it over the next month.

3. **Set an Inside-Out Goal:** Focus on achieving a measurable internal milestone, such as improving employee satisfaction or increasing efficiency.

Key Takeaway

An inside-out mindset shifts focus from reacting to external forces to building strength from within. By prioritizing your internal values, resources, and capabilities, you create a solid foundation for long-term success.

Chapter 38: Counter Aggression with Calm Confidence

When faced with aggression — whether from competitors, adversaries, or even colleagues — it's tempting to respond in kind. However, reacting emotionally often leads to poor decisions and escalates conflict. Calm confidence is a far more effective response, allowing you to maintain control, project strength, and make calculated moves.

Calm confidence doesn't mean ignoring aggression or passively accepting challenges. Instead, it involves recognizing the underlying emotions and motives driving the aggression and addressing them with composure. This approach defuses tension, shifts power dynamics, and positions you as a leader who cannot be rattled.

Why Calm Confidence is Effective

1. **Disarms Aggressors:** Aggressive individuals or competitors often expect an emotional response. Your calmness surprises and unsettles them.

2. **Maintains Control:** Staying composed ensures you act strategically rather than impulsively.

3. **Earns Respect:** Confidence without aggression demonstrates strength and maturity, earning you credibility and trust.

For example, in negotiations, an aggressive party might use pressure tactics to force concessions. Responding with calm, firm counterarguments shifts the dynamic, signaling that you won't be intimidated.

How to Counter Aggression with Calm Confidence

1. **Pause Before Reacting:** Take a moment to assess the situation and control your emotions before responding.

2. **Acknowledge Their Position:** Validating their concerns or frustrations can defuse tension and open the door for constructive dialogue.

3. **Speak with Authority:** Use clear, measured language to assert your position without escalating the conflict.

4. **Stay Focused on Your Goals:** Keep the bigger picture in mind, avoiding distractions from your core objectives.

5. **Use Non-Verbal Cues:** Maintain steady eye contact, a relaxed posture, and controlled gestures to convey calmness.

Real-World Example

During the Cuban Missile Crisis in 1962, U.S. President John F. Kennedy exemplified calm confidence in the face of Soviet aggression. While military advisors pushed for immediate, aggressive action, Kennedy chose a measured approach, engaging in strategic communication and back-channel negotiations.

This calm, calculated response prevented a nuclear confrontation and resolved the crisis peacefully, solidifying Kennedy's reputation as a thoughtful and decisive leader.

Exercises

1. **Practice Delayed Reaction:** In your next high-pressure interaction, take a moment to pause and breathe before responding. Reflect on how this affects the outcome.

2. **Build Confidence:** Identify one area where you feel uncertain. Take steps to build knowledge or skills, so you can address future challenges with greater assurance.

3. **Reflect on Past Aggression:** Think of a time you responded emotionally to aggression. How could a calm, confident approach have improved the situation?

Key Takeaway

Countering aggression with calm confidence allows you to maintain control, disarm your opponent, and demonstrate leadership. By staying composed and focused, you turn challenges into opportunities for strength and respect.

Chapter 39: Force Your Competitors to Overextend

A classic mistake in competition is overextension — when a rival stretches their resources, capabilities, or focus too thin in an attempt to achieve too much. By strategically creating situations that pressure your competitors to overcommit, you can weaken their position while conserving your own resources. This approach doesn't just exploit your rival's ambition; it transforms their strengths into liabilities.

Forcing competitors to overextend requires understanding their priorities, identifying where they're vulnerable, and setting traps that encourage them to take on more than they can handle. This can be achieved through competitive pricing, rapid innovation, or creating scenarios that compel your rivals to chase unsustainable goals.

Why Forcing Overextension Works

1. **Weakens Focus:** Overextended competitors lose clarity, making mistakes and neglecting key priorities.

2. **Exhausts Resources:** Stretching too far depletes financial, human, or operational resources, leaving rivals vulnerable.
3. **Creates Vulnerabilities:** Rivals distracted by overextension often leave critical areas exposed, giving you opportunities to strike.

For example, a company might launch multiple new products simultaneously, forcing competitors to divide their attention and resources across various fronts.

How to Force Overextension

1. **Identify Ambitious Rivals:** Overextension is most likely when competitors are overly ambitious or driven by the fear of falling behind.
2. **Create Competitive Pressure:** Introduce challenges that require significant investments of time, money, or energy to address.
3. **Encourage Missteps:** Subtly validate their ambitious moves, nudging them to overcommit to unrealistic goals.
4. **Stay Disciplined:** While your competitor stretches themselves thin, maintain focus on your core strengths and priorities.
5. **Exploit Weak Points:** As your rival overextends, identify and target areas where they've lost focus or weakened their defenses.

Real-World Example

During the Cola Wars of the 1980s, PepsiCo strategically forced Coca-Cola to overextend through aggressive marketing and new product launches. Pepsi's *Pepsi Challenge* campaign successfully portrayed its product as the preferred cola in blind taste tests, which pressured Coca-Cola to respond.

In reaction, Coca-Cola made a bold and costly move by introducing "New Coke," an updated formula intended to outshine Pepsi. The backlash from consumers, loyal to the original Coke formula, forced Coca-Cola to reintroduce "Coca-Cola Classic" just months later. This overextension of resources and focus not only strained Coca-Cola financially but also damaged its brand image temporarily, allowing Pepsi to gain ground in the market.

Exercises

1. **Analyze a Competitor:** Identify a rival who may be overextending. What are their weaknesses, and how could you apply pressure to exploit them?

2. **Test Competitive Pressure:** Create a situation that encourages a competitor to commit more resources than necessary. How do they respond?

3. **Avoid Overextension Yourself:** Reflect on areas where you might be stretching too thin. What steps can you take to refocus and strengthen your position?

Key Takeaway

Forcing competitors to overextend transforms their ambition into a liability. By creating pressure and staying focused, you weaken your rivals while conserving your own resources for strategic gains.

Chapter 40: Apply the Minimax Principle in Critical Decisions

The Minimax principle, a cornerstone of game theory, is a decision-making strategy that focuses on minimizing the maximum possible loss. In competitive environments, it helps you make critical decisions by preparing for the worst-case scenario while positioning yourself to capitalize on the best outcomes.

The goal isn't to avoid risk entirely but to ensure that even if things go wrong, the damage is manageable. This disciplined approach allows you to act with confidence, knowing you've accounted for potential downsides. The Minimax principle is particularly valuable in high-stakes situations, where uncertainty and risk are unavoidable.

Why the Minimax Principle is Powerful

1. **Reduces Vulnerability:** Preparing for worst-case scenarios protects you from catastrophic failures.

2. **Enhances Decision Clarity:** By focusing on minimizing losses, you simplify complex choices.
3. **Balances Risk and Reward:** The principle ensures you remain cautious while still pursuing opportunities.

For example, in negotiations, the Minimax principle might involve securing a fallback option or setting a clear minimum threshold to avoid walking away empty-handed.

How to Apply the Minimax Principle

1. **Define the Worst Case:** Identify the maximum loss or setback you could face in the situation.
2. **Evaluate Options:** Analyze each decision based on how it minimizes the worst possible outcome.
3. **Prepare Safeguards:** Develop contingency plans to mitigate risks and ensure stability.
4. **Act Strategically:** Once you've minimized losses, focus on maximizing potential gains without taking unnecessary risks.
5. **Adapt to New Information:** Continuously assess your decisions as new data emerges, adjusting your approach as needed.

Real-World Example

In 2008, during the global financial crisis, Berkshire Hathaway, under the leadership of Warren Buffett, applied the Minimax principle when investing in struggling companies. Rather than taking aggressive, high-risk positions, Buffett focused on minimizing potential losses while still securing gains.

One notable move was Berkshire's investment in Goldman Sachs. Buffett negotiated a deal to purchase $5 billion in preferred stock, which paid a 10% dividend and included warrants to buy common stock at a fixed price. This structure minimized Berkshire's downside risk (ensuring consistent returns from dividends) while still providing upside potential through the warrants.

This cautious yet opportunistic approach allowed Berkshire Hathaway to profit significantly from the recovery without exposing itself to undue financial risk, exemplifying the Minimax principle in action.

Exercises

1. **Identify a Critical Decision:** Write down a high-stakes decision you're currently facing. What is the worst-case scenario, and how can you minimize its impact?

2. **Develop a Contingency Plan:** Choose one area of risk and outline steps to protect yourself if the worst happens.

3. **Evaluate Past Decisions:** Reflect on a decision where you failed to consider the worst case. How could applying the Minimax principle have improved the outcome?

Key Takeaway

The Minimax principle helps you navigate uncertainty by minimizing potential losses while positioning yourself for success. By preparing for the worst and striving for the best, you make smarter, more confident decisions in competitive environments.

Part 3: Cooperative Strategies

In the competitive world of strategy, collaboration can often be the key to unlocking greater opportunities and achieving success. This section focuses on the art of cooperation — how to build trust, create value together, and sustain productive relationships while protecting your interests. Whether forming alliances, leading teams, or negotiating partnerships, these strategies will help you navigate the complexities of working with others. Cooperation isn't just about compromise; it's about crafting mutually beneficial outcomes while maintaining strength and integrity.

Chapter 41: Lay the Foundation for Trust Before You Request Collaboration

Trust is the currency of effective collaboration. Without trust, even the most promising partnerships can falter under the weight of doubt and miscommunication. Building trust before asking for collaboration ensures that the foundation of your relationship is strong, enabling smoother teamwork and more successful outcomes.

Establishing trust doesn't happen overnight. It requires consistent actions, clear communication, and a demonstrated commitment to shared values. When trust is in place, others are more willing to work with you, share resources, and take risks, knowing that the relationship is built on reliability and mutual respect.

Why Trust is Crucial in Collaboration

1. **Facilitates Open Communication:** Trust encourages honesty, reducing misunderstandings and fostering transparency.

2. **Reduces Friction:** When trust exists, disagreements are easier to resolve, as both parties believe in each other's good intentions.

3. **Strengthens Commitment:** People are more likely to invest in a partnership when they feel secure in the relationship.

For example, an entrepreneur looking to secure funding from investors must first build trust by demonstrating competence, reliability, and a shared vision for success.

How to Build Trust Before Collaboration

1. **Be Consistent:** Show reliability through your actions, delivering on promises consistently over time.

2. **Demonstrate Competence:** Prove that you have the skills and expertise to contribute effectively to the partnership.

3. **Show Empathy:** Understand the other party's goals, values, and concerns, and align your actions with their interests.

4. **Be Transparent:** Share information openly to eliminate doubts and foster confidence in your intentions.

5. **Start Small:** Build trust incrementally through smaller interactions before asking for larger commitments.

Real-World Example

In the 2000s, Procter & Gamble (P&G) established trust with smaller research firms and independent innovators before requesting collaboration through its "Connect + Develop" initiative. By actively engaging with external partners, sharing clear guidelines, and honoring intellectual property agreements, P&G demonstrated its reliability and commitment to fairness.

This foundation of trust allowed P&G to form productive partnerships that resulted in successful products such as the

Swiffer and Crest Whitestrips. By proving themselves as a trustworthy collaborator, P&G attracted top innovators and fostered long-term relationships that benefited all parties.

Exercises

1. **Evaluate Trust Levels:** Identify a relationship where you want to collaborate. What actions can you take to build trust before making your request?

2. **Reflect on Past Successes:** Think of a successful partnership in your life. What trust-building steps contributed to its success?

3. **Start Small:** Plan a small action or project that demonstrates your reliability to a potential collaborator.

Key Takeaway

Trust is the foundation of collaboration. By building trust early through consistency, transparency, and empathy, you create a strong base for productive partnerships.

Chapter 42: Bolster Mutual Dependence in Joint Ventures

MUTUAL DEPENDENCE

Mutual dependence is the glue that holds joint ventures together. When both parties rely on each other to achieve shared success, the partnership becomes stronger and more sustainable. This dynamic ensures that each partner remains committed to the venture, knowing their own success depends on the other's contributions.

In joint ventures, mutual dependence creates balance. It discourages one party from exploiting the other and fosters a sense of shared responsibility. The key is to structure the partnership so that each party's strengths complement the other's, creating a synergy that benefits both sides equally.

Why Mutual Dependence is Essential

1. **Ensures Commitment:** Partners who depend on each other are less likely to abandon the venture or act against its interests.

2. **Enhances Stability:** A balanced reliance creates equilibrium, reducing power imbalances and fostering cooperation.

3. **Maximizes Value:** Mutual dependence leverages the unique strengths of each partner, driving greater results together than either could achieve alone.

For instance, in a technology joint venture, one company might specialize in hardware development while the other focuses on software. Each party depends on the other to deliver their part of the solution, ensuring cooperation.

How to Bolster Mutual Dependence

1. **Define Clear Roles:** Assign responsibilities that highlight each partner's strengths and create interdependence.

2. **Align Incentives:** Ensure that both parties benefit equally from the venture's success.

3. **Share Resources:** Pool resources, such as funding, expertise, or technology, to deepen the partnership's value.

4. **Maintain Open Communication:** Regular updates and discussions help reinforce trust and ensure alignment.

5. **Prepare for Challenges:** Develop joint contingency plans to address potential risks or setbacks together.

Real-World Example

In 2019, Starbucks partnered with Nestlé to expand its global reach in the coffee market. Starbucks relied on Nestlé's extensive distribution network to sell its products in grocery stores worldwide, while Nestlé leveraged Starbucks' brand recognition to enhance its portfolio. This mutual dependence created a highly successful venture, with both companies benefiting from their combined strengths.

Exercises

1. **Assess a Joint Venture:** Identify a partnership or collaboration you're part of. How can you strengthen mutual dependence to ensure its success?

2. **Map Complementary Strengths:** In a current or potential partnership, list each party's unique strengths. How can these be aligned to create interdependence?

3. **Address Imbalances:** Reflect on past collaborations. Were there imbalances in dependence? What steps could have been taken to correct them?

Key Takeaway

Mutual dependence is the cornerstone of successful joint ventures. By aligning strengths, sharing responsibilities, and fostering balanced reliance, you create partnerships that are resilient and productive.

Chapter 43: Share the Pie to Make It Bigger

In many situations, competition centers on dividing a limited "pie" of resources, profits, or opportunities. However, truly successful collaboration shifts the focus from dividing the pie to making it bigger. By working together to create additional value, all parties benefit more than they would have by competing for a fixed portion.

This principle is about abundance, not scarcity. Instead of seeing collaboration as a zero-sum game, recognize that joint efforts often lead to exponential gains. Whether it's through co-developing a product, pooling resources, or sharing expertise, expanding the pie unlocks opportunities for everyone involved.

Why Expanding the Pie is Effective

1. **Maximizes Mutual Benefits:** When the pie grows, everyone gets a larger share, reducing conflict over limited resources.

2. **Fosters Innovation:** Collaboration encourages creative solutions that wouldn't arise in isolation.
3. **Builds Long-Term Partnerships:** A focus on shared growth strengthens trust and goodwill between collaborators.

For instance, companies in the same industry might partner to develop industry standards, expanding the overall market and benefiting all players.

How to Expand the Pie

1. **Focus on Value Creation:** Look for ways to add value to the collaboration rather than focusing solely on dividing existing resources.
2. **Leverage Complementary Strengths:** Combine unique assets or expertise to create synergies that neither party could achieve alone.
3. **Communicate Openly:** Share ideas and goals transparently to identify opportunities for mutual growth.
4. **Prioritize Long-Term Gains:** Aim for sustainable benefits rather than short-term wins.
5. **Celebrate Joint Successes:** Recognize and reward the shared accomplishments to reinforce the value of collaboration.

Real-World Example

In 2004, Toyota and BMW partnered to develop hydrogen fuel cell technology. Instead of competing directly, the two automakers combined their expertise—Toyota contributed its knowledge of fuel cell systems, while BMW brought its advanced materials and engineering capabilities.

By collaborating, the companies expanded the pie, accelerating the development of sustainable technology and sharing the benefits of reduced costs and enhanced innovation. This partnership highlighted how working together can unlock opportunities that would be harder to achieve individually.

Exercises

1. **Identify Collaborative Opportunities:** Think of a situation where you're competing for resources or recognition. How could collaboration create more value for everyone?

2. **Find Complementary Strengths:** Write down a potential partner's unique assets and how they align with your own to expand the pie.

3. **Focus on Shared Gains:** Reflect on a past collaboration. How could you have shifted the focus from dividing resources to creating more value together?

Key Takeaway

Sharing the pie to make it bigger creates opportunities for exponential growth. By focusing on collaboration and value creation, you build partnerships that benefit everyone involved.

Chapter 44: Use Reciprocity to Strengthen Relationships

Reciprocity — the practice of giving and receiving in return — is a cornerstone of strong relationships. In collaborative strategies, reciprocity strengthens bonds, fosters trust, and creates a cycle of mutual support. When you give generously and strategically, others feel compelled to respond in kind, deepening the relationship and paving the way for long-term cooperation.

Reciprocity doesn't just apply to material exchanges. It can take the form of offering support, sharing resources, or even providing valuable insights. The key is to give without expecting an immediate return, knowing that your generosity will likely lead to future opportunities.

Why Reciprocity Works

1. **Builds Trust:** Acts of giving demonstrate goodwill and reliability, fostering deeper connections.

2. **Creates Mutual Support:** Reciprocity ensures that both parties contribute to the relationship, balancing effort and reward.

3. **Strengthens Loyalty:** People are more likely to support those who have supported them, creating lasting partnerships.

For example, offering mentorship or guidance to a peer often leads to reciprocal opportunities, such as introductions to key contacts or collaboration on future projects.

How to Use Reciprocity Effectively

1. **Give First:** Take the initiative to offer value before asking for anything in return.

2. **Be Genuine:** Ensure your actions come from a place of authenticity, not manipulation.

3. **Match the Scale:** Tailor your contributions to the context and the relationship, ensuring they are meaningful without overextending yourself.

4. **Follow Through:** Deliver on promises to reinforce trust and demonstrate reliability.

5. **Keep the Cycle Going:** Maintain reciprocity by continuing to exchange value over time.

Real-World Example

LinkedIn's professional networking platform thrives on reciprocity. Users endorse one another's skills, share job opportunities, and provide recommendations. This cycle of giving and receiving creates stronger connections and encourages ongoing engagement, ultimately benefiting the entire LinkedIn community.

Exercises

1. **Give Without Expectation:** Identify one person in your network and offer value—whether through advice, support, or a resource—without expecting anything in return.

2. **Reflect on Reciprocity:** Think of a time when someone supported you. How did you reciprocate? How did it impact your relationship?

3. **Create a Reciprocity Plan:** List ways you can give value to key collaborators or partners in your life.

Key Takeaway

Reciprocity is the engine of strong relationships. When you give generously and authentically, you create a cycle of mutual support that strengthens partnerships and fosters long-term cooperation.

Chapter 45: Capitalize Network Effects for Influence

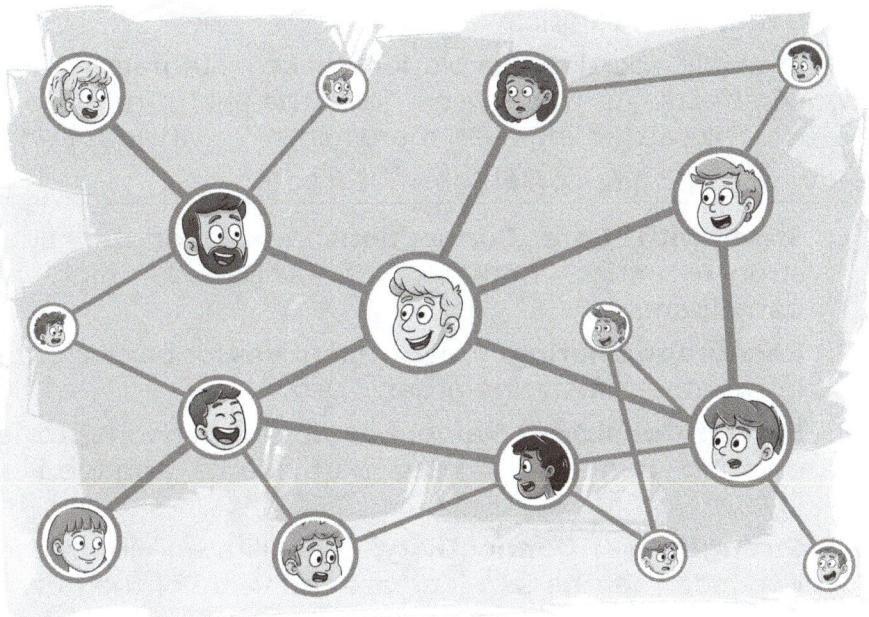

Network effects occur when the value of a product, service, or relationship increases as more people use or participate in it. In cooperative strategies, leveraging network effects allows you to expand your influence, gain access to new opportunities, and create self-sustaining growth. This concept is central to many successful platforms, ecosystems, and communities.

By building and nurturing networks, you tap into the power of collective growth. The more connections you create, the more valuable the network becomes—not just for you, but for everyone involved. This compounding value drives loyalty, participation, and engagement, amplifying your influence over time.

Why Network Effects are Powerful

1. **Create Exponential Growth:** As the network grows, so does its value, creating a self-reinforcing cycle.

2. **Increase Engagement:** Networks encourage participants to stay involved, knowing they benefit more as the network expands.

3. **Strengthen Influence:** A strong network positions you as a central figure, enhancing your ability to lead and direct opportunities.

For example, social media platforms like Instagram thrive on network effects. As more users join, the platform becomes more valuable, attracting even more users in a virtuous cycle.

How to Capitalize on Network Effects

1. **Start with Core Connections:** Focus on building a strong initial network of engaged, high-value participants.

2. **Encourage Sharing:** Create incentives for participants to invite others, fostering organic growth.

3. **Deliver Consistent Value:** Ensure the network provides ongoing benefits to keep participants engaged and loyal.

4. **Strengthen Connectivity:** Facilitate interactions between members to increase the value of the network as a whole.

5. **Adapt and Expand:** Continuously evolve the network to meet changing needs and attract new participants.

Real-World Example

Uber effectively leveraged network effects to dominate the ride-hailing industry. By focusing on onboarding more drivers, Uber ensured that riders could get faster service. In turn, the growing number of riders attracted even more drivers to the platform.

This mutually reinforcing cycle created a better experience for both parties. Riders enjoyed shorter wait times, and drivers benefited from increased demand. Uber's ability to capitalize on these network effects allowed it to outpace competitors and establish itself as the leading ride-hailing service in markets worldwide.

Exercises

1. **Map Your Network:** Identify the key connections in your professional or personal network. How can you strengthen or expand these relationships?

2. **Create Network Growth:** Develop a strategy to encourage others to join or engage with your network.

3. **Deliver Value:** Identify one way to provide consistent benefits to your network members, ensuring they remain engaged.

Key Takeaway

Network effects amplify your influence and growth by creating compounding value as more participants join. By building and nurturing networks, you position yourself as a central figure in a thriving ecosystem.

Chapter 46: Be Predictable in Cooperative Settings

Predictability might seem like a weakness in competitive settings, but in cooperation, it's a strength. Being predictable in your actions, decisions, and commitments fosters trust, reduces misunderstandings, and makes it easier for others to align with you. When collaborators know what to expect from you, they are more likely to rely on and invest in the partnership.

In cooperative environments, unpredictability creates confusion and mistrust. Partners may hesitate to commit fully if they fear you'll change direction unexpectedly. By contrast, predictability signals dependability, allowing teams and alliances to function smoothly and achieve shared goals.

Why Predictability Matters in Cooperation

1. **Builds Trust:** Consistent behavior reassures others that you will follow through on your commitments.

2. **Facilitates Planning:** When others can anticipate your actions, they can coordinate their efforts more effectively.

3. **Reduces Conflict:** Predictability minimizes the risk of misunderstandings or misaligned expectations.

For example, a project manager who consistently communicates timelines and meets deadlines creates an environment where team members can focus on their tasks without uncertainty.

How to Be Predictable in Cooperative Settings

1. **Set Clear Expectations:** Define your goals, responsibilities, and boundaries from the outset.

2. **Communicate Regularly:** Keep collaborators informed about your progress and any changes to the plan.

3. **Honor Commitments:** Follow through on promises and deliverables without fail.

4. **Develop Routines:** Establish consistent practices that signal reliability, such as weekly updates or structured meetings.

5. **Admit Mistakes Transparently:** When setbacks occur, address them openly to maintain trust.

Real-World Example

FedEx built its reputation as a dependable logistics partner by being predictably reliable. Its slogan, "When it absolutely, positively has to be there overnight," reflects its commitment to delivering packages on time, every time. This consistency has made FedEx the go-to choice for businesses and individuals worldwide, solidifying its position as a leader in the shipping industry.

Exercises

1. **Reflect on Your Predictability:** Consider a recent collaboration. Were your actions predictable and consistent? How did this impact the partnership?

2. **Establish a Routine:** Develop a habit or process that signals reliability to your team or collaborators.

3. **Communicate Expectations:** In your next group project, clearly outline what others can expect from you and encourage them to do the same.

Key Takeaway

Predictability is a cornerstone of successful cooperation. By being consistent and reliable, you foster trust, streamline coordination, and strengthen relationships in any collaborative setting.

Chapter 47: Compromise Strategically, Not Emotionally

Compromise is often essential in cooperative settings, but not all compromises are created equal. Emotional compromises, driven by frustration, guilt, or impatience, can lead to imbalanced outcomes and regret. Strategic compromises, on the other hand, are deliberate, calculated, and aligned with your long-term goals.

The key to compromising strategically is to focus on the bigger picture. Rather than simply giving in to keep the peace or to avoid conflict, you assess the potential trade-offs and ensure that what you concede is less valuable than what you gain. By thinking long-term and maintaining your priorities, you create compromises that strengthen relationships without undermining your position.

Why Strategic Compromise is Effective

1. **Preserves Your Interests:** Thoughtful compromises ensure you don't give up anything critical to your goals.

2. **Strengthens Partnerships:** Balanced compromises build goodwill and trust in collaborative relationships.

3. **Avoids Regret:** Strategic decisions prevent the resentment that often accompanies emotional sacrifices.

For instance, during a business negotiation, offering a discount on pricing in exchange for a longer contract term creates a win-win compromise. You give up some short-term revenue but secure long-term stability.

How to Compromise Strategically

1. **Understand Your Priorities:** Know what matters most to you before entering a discussion, so you can protect your key interests.

2. **Evaluate Trade-Offs:** Assess what you're giving up versus what you're gaining. Ensure the exchange is favorable to your goals.

3. **Communicate Clearly:** Articulate your reasoning to the other party, ensuring transparency and reducing misunderstandings.

4. **Stay Calm and Focused:** Avoid making decisions based on frustration or emotional pressure. Take time to think.

5. **Seek Reciprocity:** Ensure that any compromise you make is matched by a concession from the other party.

Real-World Example

The U.S. government's 2012 negotiations with auto manufacturers to improve fuel efficiency standards illustrate strategic compromise. The automakers agreed to higher standards, which aligned with environmental goals, in exchange for a gradual implementation timeline. This allowed the industry to adjust and innovate while still meeting long-term regulatory objectives.

By focusing on mutual benefits and avoiding an emotional standoff, both sides reached a compromise that advanced their priorities without unnecessary conflict.

Exercises

1. **Identify Non-Negotiables:** Write down your top three priorities in a current or upcoming negotiation. How can you protect these while remaining flexible elsewhere?

2. **Evaluate a Past Compromise:** Reflect on a time when you made a compromise. Was it strategic or emotional? What could you have done differently?

3. **Plan a Strategic Trade-Off:** Consider an area where you might need to compromise. What could you offer that costs you little but benefits the other party significantly?

Key Takeaway

Compromising strategically ensures that your decisions are thoughtful, balanced, and aligned with your goals. By focusing on long-term benefits and avoiding emotional sacrifices, you strengthen relationships without weakening your position.

Chapter 48: Maximize Joint Gains in Team-Ups

In any collaboration, the true measure of success isn't how much one party benefits — it's how much both parties gain together. Maximizing joint gains means identifying and leveraging shared opportunities to create the greatest possible value for everyone involved. This mindset goes beyond transactional thinking, fostering deeper partnerships and long-term growth.

Maximizing joint gains requires focusing on synergy: combining resources, ideas, or strengths in ways that amplify results. It also involves open communication and mutual understanding, ensuring that both parties' goals are respected and aligned. When done effectively, team-ups become a force multiplier, delivering outcomes far greater than either party could achieve alone.

Why Maximizing Joint Gains is Important

1. **Enhances Value Creation:** Shared effort and resources generate results that benefit everyone.
2. **Strengthens Partnerships:** Equitable collaboration fosters trust and encourages future cooperation.
3. **Avoids Conflict:** A focus on mutual benefit reduces competition within the partnership.

For example, two businesses collaborating on a marketing campaign can combine their audiences, expertise, and budgets to achieve greater reach and impact than either could alone.

How to Maximize Joint Gains

1. **Align Goals:** Clearly define shared objectives at the start of the collaboration to ensure mutual focus.
2. **Leverage Complementary Strengths:** Identify and utilize each party's unique resources or expertise.
3. **Encourage Open Communication:** Create an environment where both parties feel comfortable sharing ideas and feedback.
4. **Measure Success Together:** Establish metrics that reflect the shared value created by the partnership.
5. **Celebrate Joint Achievements:** Acknowledge and reward the contributions of all parties to reinforce the value of the team-up.

Real-World Example

In 2018, McDonald's and Coca-Cola collaborated on the "Sip. Share. Win!" campaign, which combined Coca-Cola's beverages with McDonald's food promotions. Customers could purchase specially marked Coca-Cola beverages at McDonald's and enter for a chance to win prizes, including free McDonald's meals.

This team-up benefited both brands: McDonald's boosted customer traffic while Coca-Cola strengthened its association with a major food retailer. By aligning their marketing efforts and leveraging their mutual popularity, the partnership created greater engagement and value for both companies and their customers.

Exercises

1. **Identify Shared Goals:** Think of a current or potential partnership. What mutual objectives could you align to create greater value?

2. **Leverage Complementary Skills:** List the unique strengths you and a collaborator bring to the table. How can you combine them for maximum impact?

3. **Evaluate Success Metrics:** Define how you'll measure the joint success of a collaboration. How do these metrics benefit both parties equally?

Key Takeaway

Maximizing joint gains transforms partnerships into high-value opportunities. By aligning goals, leveraging strengths, and creating shared success, you build collaborations that deliver exponential results for everyone involved.

Chapter 49: Establish Harmony Between Transparency and Secrecy

In collaborative efforts, striking the right balance between transparency and secrecy is vital. Transparency builds trust, aligns goals, and facilitates teamwork, while secrecy safeguards your competitive edge and protects sensitive information. Navigating this balance requires a strategic approach that considers the context, the partners involved, and the ultimate objectives of the collaboration.

When too much is revealed, you risk exposing vulnerabilities or losing your unique advantage. Conversely, excessive secrecy can breed suspicion, misunderstandings, or even conflicts. Finding the harmony between these extremes ensures that the partnership is both effective and secure.

This balance is particularly important in high-stakes collaborations, such as mergers, product co-developments, or strategic alliances. By sharing enough information to foster alignment while withholding details that could compromise your position, you create an environment of trust and protection.

Why Balancing Transparency and Secrecy Matters

1. **Builds Trust:** Transparency shows good faith and commitment, encouraging others to invest in the collaboration.

2. **Enhances Cooperation:** Open communication ensures everyone is on the same page, reducing misalignment.

3. **Protects Critical Assets:** Keeping key details confidential prevents leaks, theft, or misuse of sensitive information.

Consider a startup collaborating with a larger corporation to launch a new product. The startup must share its product roadmap and development goals to ensure the partnership's success but may withhold proprietary technology or patent information to avoid losing its competitive advantage.

How to Balance Transparency and Secrecy

1. **Define Boundaries Early:** Establish clear guidelines about what information will be shared and what will remain private.

2. **Tailor Transparency Levels:** Adjust your openness based on the trustworthiness, track record, and role of each partner in the collaboration.

3. **Communicate Strategically:** Share information that directly contributes to the partnership's goals and hold back details that aren't immediately relevant.

4. **Use Legal Protections:** Non-disclosure agreements (NDAs) and confidentiality clauses ensure that shared information remains secure.

5. **Monitor Continuously:** Assess the effectiveness of your balance over time and adapt as the partnership evolves.

Real-World Example

In the pharmaceutical industry, companies frequently collaborate to develop drugs or vaccines, such as Pfizer and BioNTech's partnership during the COVID-19 pandemic. The two companies shared vital research data and aligned their production goals while protecting their proprietary technologies. This balance allowed both parties to work effectively toward their shared objective without compromising their individual competitive positions.

Exercises

1. **Assess Your Current Approach:** In an existing partnership, evaluate whether you're being too transparent or overly secretive. Adjust your strategy accordingly.

2. **Create a Sharing Framework:** Outline specific types of information you're willing to share in collaborations and what must remain confidential.

3. **Seek Feedback:** Ask collaborators if they feel your level of transparency fosters trust and alignment. Use their input to refine your approach.

Key Takeaway

Striking the right balance between transparency and secrecy ensures effective collaboration while protecting your interests. By aligning openness with strategic confidentiality, you create partnerships that are both trustworthy and secure.

Chapter 50: Foster a Reputation for Fair Actions

In cooperative strategies, your reputation is one of your greatest assets. A reputation for fairness attracts high-quality partners, fosters loyalty, and strengthens your influence within any group. When others perceive you as someone who acts equitably and prioritizes mutual benefit, they're more likely to engage with you, invest in your success, and remain committed to long-term relationships.

Fostering a reputation for fairness doesn't happen overnight. It requires consistent, intentional actions that demonstrate ethical behavior, transparency, and respect for others' contributions. Over time, this commitment to fairness creates a lasting impression that sets you apart as a trustworthy and reliable collaborator.

Why a Reputation for Fairness Matters

1. **Builds Trust:** Fair actions signal integrity, reassuring others of your intentions and reliability.

2. **Encourages Cooperation:** People are more willing to collaborate with those they believe will treat them equitably.

3. **Enhances Influence:** A fair reputation positions you as a leader, making others more likely to follow your guidance.

For instance, leaders who consistently credit their teams for successes build goodwill and inspire greater effort, creating a positive cycle of trust and productivity.

How to Foster a Reputation for Fair Actions

1. **Act Consistently:** Ensure that your decisions reflect fairness across all situations, avoiding favoritism or bias.

2. **Communicate Your Reasoning:** Be transparent about the factors influencing your decisions to eliminate doubts or perceptions of unfairness.

3. **Acknowledge Contributions:** Publicly recognize and reward the efforts of those you work with, demonstrating your commitment to equity.

4. **Correct Mistakes Proactively:** If you've acted unfairly, address the situation immediately to rebuild trust.

5. **Promote Equity:** Strive to create opportunities that are distributed fairly among all stakeholders.

Real-World Example

Patagonia, the outdoor apparel company, exemplifies the power of fairness in business. By ensuring ethical labor practices, providing fair wages, and maintaining environmentally sustainable operations, Patagonia has built a reputation for acting with integrity. This approach has not only attracted loyal customers but also like-minded collaborators, amplifying its positive impact.

Exercises

1. **Reflect on Past Decisions:** Think of a situation where fairness may have been questioned. What steps could you take to improve similar decisions in the future?

2. **Develop a Fairness Checklist:** Create a set of criteria to evaluate the fairness of your decisions before taking action.

3. **Solicit Feedback:** Ask collaborators or team members for honest feedback on how they perceive your fairness. Use this insight to refine your actions.

Key Takeaway

A reputation for fairness is a powerful tool in cooperation. By consistently acting with integrity, transparency, and equity, you build trust and create opportunities for stronger, more productive relationships.

Chapter 51: Turn Enemies into Allies

In competitive environments, it's natural to encounter adversaries—individuals or organizations whose goals conflict with yours. While conflict can sometimes motivate innovation and progress, prolonged hostility often drains resources and limits opportunities. Transforming enemies into allies is a powerful strategy that not only neutralizes threats but also creates opportunities for collaboration and mutual growth.

Turning adversaries into allies requires understanding their goals, identifying common ground, and building trust over time. This transformation doesn't mean compromising your principles or giving up your objectives. Instead, it's about finding ways to align interests and create a win-win dynamic that benefits both parties.

Why Turning Enemies into Allies Matters

1. **Neutralizes Conflict:** Resolving hostility reduces wasted energy and resources.
2. **Creates New Opportunities:** Collaborating with former adversaries can unlock shared potential.
3. **Demonstrates Leadership:** Transforming conflict into cooperation showcases strategic foresight and emotional intelligence.

For example, two rival businesses might partner to co-develop a product that neither could create alone, leveraging each other's strengths to achieve a shared goal.

How to Turn Enemies into Allies

1. **Understand Their Perspective:** Learn your adversary's goals, motivations, and challenges. Empathy is key to finding common ground.
2. **Start Small:** Propose low-risk collaborations that build trust and demonstrate the potential for mutual benefit.
3. **Communicate Transparently:** Be honest about your intentions and goals to reduce suspicion and foster trust.
4. **Focus on Common Goals:** Highlight areas where your interests align and work together to achieve shared outcomes.
5. **Maintain Boundaries:** While fostering collaboration, ensure your core values and objectives remain intact.

Real-World Example

In 2018, Microsoft and Sony, long-time rivals in the gaming industry, surprised the market by announcing a strategic partnership to collaborate on cloud gaming and AI solutions. Historically, the two companies competed fiercely in the console wars with Xbox and PlayStation. However, the rise of cloud gaming and emerging competition from tech giants like Google and Amazon prompted them to join forces.

By collaborating on advanced technologies, Microsoft and Sony were able to strengthen their positions in the gaming ecosystem while addressing shared challenges. This partnership demonstrated how even staunch rivals can align their interests to achieve mutual benefits and tackle external threats.

Exercises

1. **Identify Potential Allies:** List current adversaries in your professional or personal life. What common goals or interests could form the basis of collaboration?

2. **Propose a Small Collaboration:** Think of a low-risk way to work with a rival, such as sharing insights or co-hosting an event.

3. **Evaluate Past Conflicts:** Reflect on a previous adversarial relationship. Could it have been transformed into an alliance? How?

Key Takeaway

Turning enemies into allies transforms conflict into opportunity. By finding common ground and building trust, you neutralize threats and create partnerships that drive mutual success.

Chapter 52: Concentrate on the Shared Objective

Collaboration is most effective when everyone is aligned toward a shared objective. When goals diverge, distractions, inefficiencies, and conflicts arise, weakening the partnership's impact. Focusing on the shared objective ensures that all efforts contribute to a common purpose, maximizing efficiency and results.

This focus doesn't mean suppressing individual ideas or goals. It's about integrating them into the broader mission. By keeping the shared objective front and center, collaborators can navigate disagreements and distractions without losing sight of the ultimate purpose.

Why Focusing on the Shared Objective is Critical

1. **Enhances Alignment:** Clear goals unify efforts, ensuring that all actions support the partnership's mission.

2. **Reduces Conflict:** A common purpose minimizes disputes by providing a clear framework for decision-making.

3. **Boosts Efficiency:** Concentrating on shared outcomes streamlines processes and eliminates redundant efforts.

For instance, in a joint research project, focusing on the end goal — such as publishing a breakthrough study — helps partners prioritize tasks and allocate resources effectively.

How to Concentrate on the Shared Objective

1. **Define the Goal Clearly:** Establish a specific, measurable objective that all parties agree on.

2. **Revisit the Objective Regularly:** Keep the goal visible during discussions and decision-making to ensure alignment.

3. **Encourage Open Dialogue:** Allow team members to voice concerns or ideas, but always tie conversations back to the shared goal.

4. **Celebrate Progress Together:** Acknowledge milestones to reinforce commitment to the objective.

5. **Avoid Scope Creep:** Resist the temptation to add unrelated tasks or goals that dilute focus.

Real-World Example

The International Space Station (ISS) is a remarkable example of global collaboration focused on a shared objective. Despite political and cultural differences, space agencies from multiple countries—including NASA, Roscosmos, and ESA—united around the goal of advancing space exploration and scientific research.

By concentrating on their common mission, these agencies overcame challenges and built one of humanity's greatest scientific achievements.

Exercises

1. **Define a Shared Goal:** In a current collaboration, write down the main objective and ensure all participants are aligned with it.

2. **Refocus a Distraction:** Identify a recent discussion or task that strayed from the shared goal. How can you redirect efforts back to the main objective?

3. **Celebrate a Milestone:** Choose a recent achievement in your collaboration and acknowledge how it contributed to the shared mission.

Key Takeaway

Focusing on the shared objective ensures that collaboration is unified, efficient, and purpose-driven. By aligning efforts and minimizing distractions, you maximize the impact of your partnerships.

Chapter 53: Generate Value Before Asking for Value

In cooperative settings, trust and goodwill often hinge on your ability to demonstrate value before making requests. Generating value first shows others that you're invested in the relationship, not just seeking to benefit from it. This approach fosters trust, strengthens connections, and encourages reciprocity, creating a foundation for long-term collaboration.

Generating value doesn't always require grand gestures. It can be as simple as offering advice, sharing resources, or lending support without expecting an immediate return. These small actions accumulate, building goodwill and positioning you as a valuable and reliable partner.

Why Generating Value First is Effective

1. **Builds Trust:** Giving before asking demonstrates your commitment to the partnership.
2. **Encourages Reciprocity:** People are naturally inclined to return favors, fostering mutual benefit.

3. **Establishes Reputation:** Creating value reinforces your reliability and positions you as an asset in any collaboration.

For example, a professional networking contact who consistently shares job leads, offers mentorship, or connects others without expecting immediate payback will likely receive more support when they need it.

How to Generate Value Before Asking for Value

1. **Understand Their Needs:** Identify what your collaborators or partners value most and offer support in those areas.
2. **Offer Expertise:** Share your knowledge or skills to help others solve problems or achieve their goals.
3. **Provide Resources:** Contribute tools, information, or connections that can benefit the partnership.
4. **Be Proactive:** Look for opportunities to create value without waiting to be asked.
5. **Stay Consistent:** Continue offering value over time to build a strong, enduring relationship.

Real-World Example

In the early days of HubSpot, the company built its reputation by offering free educational content and tools to businesses, such as blogs, webinars, and marketing resources. This approach demonstrated HubSpot's expertise and commitment to helping businesses grow, even before they became paying customers.

By creating value upfront, HubSpot earned the trust of its audience and established itself as a leader in inbound marketing. This value-first strategy not only attracted loyal customers but also laid the foundation for long-term relationships, ensuring continued success as the company grew.

Exercises

1. **Identify an Opportunity to Give:** Think of a relationship where you could create value without expecting anything in return. Take one small action this week.

2. **Reflect on Reciprocity:** Consider a time when someone created value for you. How did it affect your willingness to support them later?

3. **Plan a Value-First Approach:** In an upcoming collaboration or negotiation, outline ways you can contribute before making requests.

Key Takeaway

Generating value first builds trust, fosters goodwill, and lays the groundwork for productive partnerships. By investing in others, you position yourself as a reliable and valuable collaborator.

Chapter 54: Be Generous Without Being Exploitable

Generosity is a powerful tool in collaboration, but unchecked generosity can lead to exploitation. Being generous without being exploitable means contributing freely and meaningfully to partnerships while setting clear boundaries to protect your interests.

Generosity fosters trust, goodwill, and reciprocity, but when taken too far, it can leave you vulnerable to unfair demands or overreliance. Striking the right balance ensures that your contributions are valued and that your generosity strengthens the partnership rather than depleting your resources.

Why Balanced Generosity is Important

1. **Builds Trust:** Genuine generosity shows others that you care about the partnership's success.

2. **Encourages Fairness:** Boundaries ensure that your generosity is respected rather than taken for granted.

3. **Protects Resources:** Maintaining balance prevents burnout or overextension, ensuring your long-term effectiveness.

For instance, in a team project, offering to take on additional tasks demonstrates generosity, but agreeing to do everything can lead to resentment and imbalance.

How to Be Generous Without Being Exploitable

1. **Set Clear Boundaries:** Define what you're willing to give and where you need to draw the line.
2. **Monitor Reciprocity:** Ensure that your generosity is met with fairness and effort from the other party.
3. **Communicate Assertively:** Politely decline requests that exceed your boundaries while offering alternative support.
4. **Prioritize Meaningful Contributions:** Focus on actions that create the greatest impact for the partnership.
5. **Evaluate the Relationship:** Periodically assess whether the partnership remains equitable and beneficial.

Real-World Example

In the world of freelancing, graphic designers often offer initial consultations or sample work to attract clients. The most successful freelancers balance generosity — providing high-quality previews of their work — while setting clear boundaries, such as limiting the number of revisions or charging for additional services. This approach ensures their contributions are valued without being exploited.

Exercises

1. **Assess Your Generosity:** Reflect on a recent partnership. Were you too generous or not generous enough? What could you have done differently?
2. **Define Your Boundaries:** Write down your limits for time, effort, or resources in collaborations. Practice communicating them assertively.
3. **Track Reciprocity:** In an ongoing collaboration, evaluate whether the relationship is balanced. Take steps to restore fairness if needed.

Key Takeaway

Generosity builds trust and goodwill, but it must be balanced with clear boundaries to avoid exploitation. By giving freely while protecting your interests, you create stronger, more sustainable partnerships.

Chapter 55: Align Incentives to Sustain Cooperation

For cooperation to thrive, all parties involved must feel that their efforts contribute to shared success while also advancing their personal or organizational goals. Aligning incentives ensures that everyone has a clear, mutual reason to stay committed to the partnership, reducing conflict and fostering long-term collaboration.

Misaligned incentives often lead to misunderstandings, inefficiencies, and even resentment, as parties may prioritize their own interests over the group's objectives. By carefully structuring agreements and understanding what motivates each participant, you can create an environment where collaboration feels natural and rewarding.

Why Aligning Incentives is Critical

1. **Fosters Commitment:** Shared benefits keep all parties engaged and invested in the partnership.

2. **Reduces Conflict:** When goals are aligned, there's less competition within the collaboration.

3. **Enhances Productivity:** Clear incentives encourage each party to contribute their best efforts.

For example, in a business joint venture, offering equity shares tied to performance ensures that all parties have a vested interest in achieving success.

How to Align Incentives

1. **Understand Motivations:** Identify what each participant values most, whether it's financial rewards, recognition, or creative freedom.

2. **Create Win-Win Structures:** Design agreements where success for one party directly benefits the others.

3. **Set Clear Metrics:** Define measurable goals and rewards tied to specific outcomes.

4. **Revisit Agreements Regularly:** Ensure that incentives remain fair and relevant as the partnership evolves.

5. **Acknowledge Contributions:** Regularly recognize and reward individual efforts to maintain morale and motivation.

Real-World Example

The partnership between Lego and Universal Music Group (UMG) in 2020 demonstrates the importance of aligned incentives. The two companies collaborated to create LEGO VIDIYO, a product line that combined Lego's creativity and UMG's music catalog to allow kids to create music videos using physical bricks and augmented reality.

The incentives were perfectly aligned: Lego gained access to popular music to enhance its product appeal, while UMG introduced its artists to a younger audience. Both parties benefited from the collaboration, encouraging sustained cooperation as the product developed and expanded.

Exercises

1. **Evaluate a Current Partnership:** Identify whether the incentives in your collaboration are aligned. How could they be improved?

2. **Design a Win-Win Model:** In a new or potential partnership, outline how both parties can benefit equally from shared success.

3. **Monitor Incentive Impact:** Reflect on how current incentives influence behavior within your team or collaboration. Adjust if necessary.

Key Takeaway

Aligned incentives sustain cooperation by ensuring that everyone benefits from shared success. By understanding motivations and creating win-win structures, you foster long-term, productive relationships.

Chapter 56: Honor Loyalty Proactively

Loyalty is the cornerstone of lasting relationships, but it must be nurtured and rewarded to remain strong. Honoring loyalty proactively means not waiting until someone questions their commitment to you. Instead, it involves consistently recognizing and appreciating their efforts, contributions, or allegiance, ensuring they feel valued and motivated to maintain the relationship.

Proactive loyalty doesn't just strengthen bonds—it also reinforces your reputation as a trustworthy partner. This approach minimizes turnover in teams, discourages opportunistic behavior in collaborations, and fosters a culture of mutual respect and support.

Why Honoring Loyalty Matters

1. **Strengthens Relationships:** Recognizing loyalty deepens trust and commitment.

2. **Encourages Reciprocity:** Loyal actions inspire similar dedication from others.
3. **Enhances Stability:** Loyal collaborators are less likely to seek alternative opportunities, ensuring continuity.

For instance, employers who regularly acknowledge and reward long-term employees through promotions, bonuses, or public recognition often see higher retention rates and improved morale.

How to Honor Loyalty Proactively

1. **Show Appreciation:** Regularly thank collaborators for their contributions and dedication.
2. **Offer Tangible Rewards:** Provide meaningful benefits, such as financial bonuses, new opportunities, or public recognition.
3. **Create Growth Opportunities:** Ensure loyal partners or team members have chances to advance or expand their skills.
4. **Communicate Openly:** Keep loyal collaborators informed about changes or plans to make them feel included and valued.
5. **Be Consistent:** Demonstrate loyalty in return by standing by your collaborators in times of uncertainty or challenge.

Real-World Example

Loyalty programs in hospitality, such as Marriott Bonvoy, exemplify proactive loyalty. Marriott consistently rewards frequent customers with points, upgrades, and exclusive perks, reinforcing their commitment to the brand. This proactive recognition ensures that loyal customers feel valued and remain engaged, leading to long-term relationships and repeat business.

Exercises

1. **Identify Loyal Partners:** List individuals or groups who have shown consistent loyalty to you or your organization. What steps can you take to honor their commitment?

2. **Plan a Loyalty Reward:** Develop a meaningful way to recognize and reward loyalty in your personal or professional life.

3. **Reflect on Reciprocity:** Think about how you demonstrate loyalty in return. Are there areas where you could improve?

Key Takeaway

Honoring loyalty proactively strengthens relationships, fosters trust, and encourages long-term commitment. By consistently recognizing and rewarding dedication, you build a foundation of mutual respect and shared success.

Chapter 57: Forge Coalitions Around Shared Interests

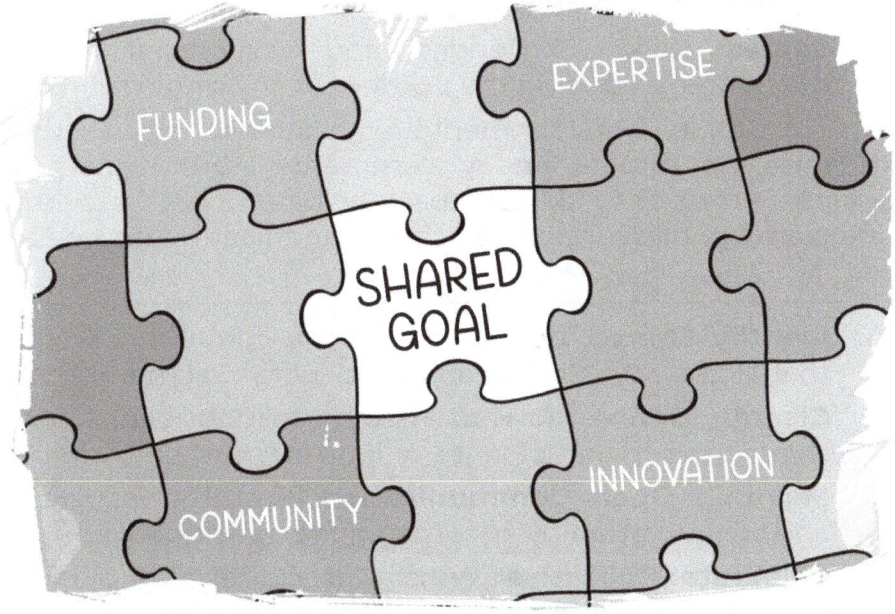

Forging coalitions can be the key to achieving goals that might otherwise be out of reach. Coalitions are alliances of individuals or organizations united by common interests, where each member contributes their strengths to the group's collective success. By pooling resources, knowledge, and influence, coalitions amplify impact and create opportunities for mutual growth.

The key to successful coalitions lies in identifying shared interests that motivate all members equally. A strong coalition isn't just about joining forces—it's about ensuring that every participant benefits meaningfully from the collaboration. By focusing on common ground and clearly defining roles, you create an alliance that thrives on trust, respect, and a shared vision.

Why Forging Coalitions is Powerful

1. **Combines Strengths:** Coalitions bring together diverse resources, skills, and perspectives for greater impact.
2. **Builds Credibility:** Working as a united front increases influence and legitimacy.
3. **Shares Risk:** Challenges and responsibilities are distributed, reducing the burden on any single member.

For example, environmental coalitions often unite companies, non-profits, and governments around goals like reducing emissions. These partnerships pool expertise, funding, and public support to achieve significant outcomes.

How to Forge Effective Coalitions

1. **Identify Shared Goals:** Focus on a common objective that aligns with the interests of all potential members.
2. **Clearly Define Roles:** Assign responsibilities that leverage each participant's unique strengths.
3. **Maintain Open Communication:** Foster transparency and collaboration by encouraging regular dialogue.
4. **Celebrate Collective Wins:** Recognize and publicize successes to reinforce the coalition's value.
5. **Adapt to Change:** Be flexible and willing to adjust strategies as new opportunities or challenges arise.

Real-World Example

The Fair Trade Movement is a prime example of coalitions built around shared interests. Fairtrade International brings together farmers, workers, businesses, and NGOs with the common goal of promoting sustainable agriculture and ethical trading practices.

By pooling resources and aligning their efforts, this coalition has empowered small-scale farmers, improved working conditions, and raised awareness about ethical consumption worldwide. The coalition's success demonstrates how diverse groups with complementary strengths can unite to achieve significant, shared objectives that benefit all members.

Exercises

1. **Identify a Common Goal:** Think of a challenge or opportunity where collaboration could amplify success. Who might share your interests?

2. **Build a Coalition Plan:** Outline the key stakeholders, their potential contributions, and how they might benefit from joining your coalition.

3. **Evaluate a Past Collaboration:** Reflect on a previous group effort. What worked well, and what could have been improved?

Key Takeaway

Coalitions built around shared interests create powerful synergies. When you unite diverse strengths and focusing on common goals, you amplify impact and achieve outcomes that benefit all members.

Chapter 58: Avoid Overpromising in Groups

The desire to please others or secure agreement can lead to overpromising — making commitments that are unrealistic or unsustainable. While well-intentioned, overpromising often results in missed deadlines, strained relationships, and diminished trust when expectations aren't met.

Avoiding overpromising doesn't mean being overly cautious or unambitious. Instead, it's about being realistic, honest, and transparent about what you can deliver. By managing expectations effectively, you ensure that your contributions are reliable and that the group maintains confidence in your commitments.

Why Avoiding Overpromising is Essential

1. **Preserves Trust:** Meeting expectations consistently reinforces credibility and reliability.
2. **Reduces Stress:** Realistic commitments prevent overwork and burnout.

3. **Promotes Long-Term Success:** Sustainable efforts lead to stronger, more enduring relationships.

For instance, in project collaborations, committing to an unachievable timeline can disrupt the entire group's workflow. Setting a realistic schedule ensures smoother coordination and better outcomes.

How to Avoid Overpromising

1. **Be Honest About Capacity:** Assess your resources, time, and abilities before making commitments.
2. **Set Realistic Expectations:** Clearly communicate what you can and cannot deliver.
3. **Provide Updates:** If challenges arise, inform the group promptly and adjust expectations as needed.
4. **Focus on Quality Over Quantity:** Commit to fewer tasks, but execute them to the highest standard.
5. **Learn From Experience:** Reflect on past commitments to identify patterns and improve future decision-making.

Real-World Example

In the automotive industry, Ford provides a valuable example of avoiding overpromising. During the launch of the all-electric Ford F-150 Lightning, Ford carefully set realistic expectations regarding delivery timelines and production capacity. Instead of overpromising on immediate availability, the company communicated a phased rollout plan and adjusted delivery schedules as demand surged.

By managing customer expectations upfront, Ford maintained trust and avoided the backlash often associated with missed promises. This approach ensured a smoother launch and strengthened its reputation as a reliable and transparent automaker.

Exercises

1. **Evaluate Your Current Commitments:** Are there any promises you've made that may be unrealistic? How can you address this proactively?
2. **Practice Saying No:** In your next group discussion, identify a request you can decline or renegotiate for clarity and balance.

3. **Reflect on Past Overpromises:** Think about a time when you overpromised. What were the consequences, and how can you improve moving forward?

Key Takeaway

Avoiding overpromising in groups safeguards trust and ensures sustainable success. This approach allows you to set realistic expectations, deliver consistently, build credibility and strengthen collaborative relationships.

Chapter 59: Communicate Clearly to Reduce Misunderstandings

Miscommunication is one of the most common barriers to effective collaboration. Unclear messages, assumptions, and ambiguity can lead to misunderstandings, delays, and even conflicts. Clear communication ensures that everyone involved in a partnership or team is aligned, informed, and able to act with confidence.

Effective communication isn't just about speaking clearly — it's about listening actively, tailoring your message to your audience, and confirming mutual understanding. When communication is prioritized, teams function more smoothly, partnerships thrive, and shared goals are more easily achieved.

Why Clear Communication is Crucial

1. **Prevents Confusion:** Clear messages reduce the likelihood of misinterpretation or errors.
2. **Builds Trust:** Transparent and honest communication fosters confidence and strengthens relationships.

3. **Enhances Efficiency:** When everyone understands their roles and responsibilities, tasks are completed more effectively.

For example, during team projects, regularly clarifying goals, deadlines, and expectations minimizes confusion and keeps progress on track.

How to Communicate Clearly

1. **Define Your Message:** Be clear about the purpose and key points of your communication before delivering it.

2. **Use Simple Language:** Avoid jargon or overly complex phrases that could confuse your audience.

3. **Confirm Understanding:** Ask for feedback or repeat key points to ensure your message has been received as intended.

4. **Adapt to Your Audience:** Tailor your tone and delivery to suit the needs and preferences of your collaborators.

5. **Be Transparent:** Share necessary details openly, avoiding omissions that could lead to misunderstandings.

Real-World Example

NASA's Apollo missions highlight the importance of clear communication. Engineers, astronauts, and mission control relied on precise and unambiguous instructions to execute complex tasks. For instance, during the Apollo 13 crisis, clear, step-by-step communication between astronauts and mission control enabled the team to safely navigate life-threatening challenges, demonstrating how effective communication can make or break a collaboration.

Exercises

1. **Audit a Recent Interaction:** Reflect on a conversation or email. Were your key points clearly conveyed? How could you improve?

2. **Practice Active Listening:** In your next meeting, focus on understanding others' perspectives fully before responding.

3. **Clarify Roles:** In your current team project, ensure that everyone understands their responsibilities by summarizing and confirming them.

Key Takeaway

Clear communication reduces misunderstandings and ensures alignment in collaborative efforts. By listening actively and delivering concise, transparent messages, you foster trust and streamline success.

Chapter 60: Exit Teams Gracefully When Necessary

Sometimes, the best decision in a collaborative effort is to step away. Exiting a team or partnership isn't inherently negative — it can signify growth, a shift in priorities, or the conclusion of your role in a project. However, how you leave a group matters significantly. Exiting gracefully ensures that relationships remain intact, reputations are preserved, and future opportunities for collaboration remain open.

A graceful exit involves honesty, professionalism, and a focus on the group's continued success. By clearly communicating your reasons and ensuring a smooth transition, you leave a positive impression and minimize disruption to the team's goals.

Why Exiting Gracefully Matters

1. **Preserves Relationships:** A positive departure maintains goodwill and future collaboration potential.

2. **Minimizes Disruption:** Planning your exit ensures continuity for the remaining team.
3. **Enhances Reputation:** A thoughtful exit demonstrates professionalism and maturity.

For instance, a project manager transitioning out of a role might document processes, train their replacement, and offer continued support during the handover.

How to Exit Teams Gracefully

1. **Communicate Early:** Inform the team of your intention to leave as soon as possible, providing sufficient notice.
2. **Explain Your Reasons:** Share your decision honestly and constructively, focusing on growth or new opportunities rather than grievances.
3. **Support the Transition:** Help identify or train a replacement, and ensure all your responsibilities are documented and delegated.
4. **Express Gratitude:** Acknowledge the team's contributions and express appreciation for the experience.
5. **Stay Open to the Future:** Keep the door open for future collaborations by leaving on positive terms.

Real-World Example

When Eric Schmidt stepped down as Google's CEO in 2011, he exemplified a graceful exit. Schmidt transitioned to an executive chairman role, ensuring a smooth handover of responsibilities to co-founder Larry Page. He continued to advise and support the company, preserving strong relationships and contributing to Google's ongoing success.

Exercises

1. **Plan a Hypothetical Exit:** Imagine leaving your current team or project. What steps would you take to ensure a smooth transition?
2. **Reflect on Past Exits:** Consider a time when you left a group or role. What went well, and what could have been handled better?

3. **Express Gratitude:** Write a note of appreciation to a current or past collaborator, strengthening your professional relationships.

Key Takeaway

Exiting teams gracefully ensures positive relationships, smooth transitions, and ongoing opportunities. By communicating openly and prioritizing the group's success, you leave a lasting, constructive impact.

Part 4: Adaptive Strategies

Adaptability is not just a skill — it's a necessity. This section explores how to thrive in unpredictable environments by staying flexible, innovative, and resilient. By mastering the art of adaptation, you'll be equipped to seize opportunities, outmaneuver challenges, and thrive no matter what the future holds.

Chapter 61: Anticipate Game-Changing Trends

Game-changing trends can disrupt industries, reshape markets, and create new opportunities for those who see them early. Anticipating these shifts allows you to stay ahead of competitors and position yourself to benefit from the coming change. It's not about predicting the future with certainty — it's about identifying patterns, analyzing signals, and preparing to act when opportunities arise.

Successful leaders and organizations make trend-watching a priority. They monitor technological advances, cultural shifts, and emerging industries to spot potential transformations. By understanding the forces driving change, you can align your strategies to harness these trends before they reshape the landscape.

Why Anticipating Trends is Critical

1. **First-Mover Advantage:** Early identification allows you to act before others, gaining a competitive edge.
2. **Reduces Risk:** Preparing for change minimizes disruption and positions you to adapt smoothly.
3. **Encourages Innovation:** Staying ahead of trends inspires forward-thinking strategies and solutions.

For instance, companies that embraced remote work technologies before the COVID-19 pandemic were better prepared to transition when the world suddenly shifted to work-from-home models.

How to Anticipate Game-Changing Trends

1. **Track Key Indicators:** Monitor industry reports, emerging technologies, and consumer behavior for early signs of change.
2. **Engage with Experts:** Participate in discussions, panels, and networks that provide insights into future developments.
3. **Analyze Adjacent Industries:** Look at trends in related fields that could impact your sector.
4. **Embrace Curiosity:** Encourage your team to explore unconventional ideas and challenge assumptions.
5. **Prepare for Multiple Scenarios:** Develop flexible plans that account for a range of possible outcomes.

Real-World Example

In the 1980s, Apple anticipated the growing demand for personal computers that were user-friendly and accessible to non-technical users. While other companies focused on technical specifications and business markets, Apple saw an opportunity to cater to everyday consumers.

The launch of the Macintosh in 1984, featuring a graphical user interface and a mouse, revolutionized the personal computing industry. This foresight into the trend toward intuitive, design-oriented technology established Apple as a leader in consumer innovation and shaped the modern tech landscape.

Exercises

1. **Identify Emerging Trends:** Write down three trends in your industry that could disrupt or transform the market.
2. **Scenario Planning:** Create a strategy for how you would adapt if one of these trends became dominant.
3. **Expand Your Horizon:** Research a field outside your industry to identify innovations that might impact your work.

Key Takeaway

Anticipating game-changing trends positions you to act before others, turning potential disruptions into opportunities. By staying curious and prepared, you can adapt and thrive in a rapidly evolving world.

Chapter 62: Be the First to Spot Weak Signals

Major shifts often begin as faint signals — early indicators of change that are easy to miss but critical to spot. Being the first to notice these weak signals allows you to act decisively, while others remain unaware or hesitant. These signals might include subtle shifts in consumer behavior, emerging technologies, or small market disruptions that hint at larger trends to come.

Spotting weak signals requires an open mind, curiosity, and a willingness to explore unconventional sources of information. It also involves interpreting the context of these signals and assessing their potential impact. Acting on weak signals is risky, but when done wisely, it positions you as a pioneer.

Why Spotting Weak Signals Matters

1. **Provides an Early Advantage:** Acting on signals before others gives you a head start.

2. **Minimizes Surprises:** Early awareness allows you to prepare for potential disruptions.

3. **Drives Innovation:** Weak signals often highlight opportunities to create or improve solutions.

For example, the rise of plant-based diets started as a weak signal with niche products like tofu and almond milk. Companies like Beyond Meat and Oatly recognized this trend early, developing innovative plant-based alternatives and growing their market before competitors.

How to Spot Weak Signals

1. **Look Beyond the Mainstream:** Explore niche markets, independent research, and emerging technologies for early indicators.

2. **Track Anomalies:** Pay attention to unexpected shifts in data, customer behavior, or market patterns.

3. **Foster Diverse Input:** Engage with individuals from different industries, cultures, or backgrounds to gain fresh perspectives.

4. **Experiment with Ideas:** Test small-scale initiatives to explore the potential of weak signals.

5. **Monitor Continuously:** Weak signals can emerge gradually, so keep an eye on trends over time.

Real-World Example

In the mid-2010s, Square (now Block, Inc.) recognized weak signals pointing to a growing demand for mobile payment solutions among small businesses. While larger payment processors focused on established retailers, Square introduced its portable card reader, enabling entrepreneurs, food trucks, and small vendors to accept credit card payments conveniently through their smartphones.

This move, based on early observations of small businesses' struggles with traditional payment systems, allowed Square to capture an underserved market segment. By acting on these weak signals, Square not only filled a critical gap but also set the stage for its long-term success in financial technology.

Exercises

1. **Identify Weak Signals:** List three subtle changes or anomalies you've noticed in your industry. What might they indicate?

2. **Explore Niche Communities:** Join forums, attend events, or follow niche influencers to uncover emerging ideas.

3. **Test a Hypothesis:** Develop a small project or initiative based on a weak signal you've identified.

Key Takeaway

Spotting weak signals allows you to act early and capitalize on emerging opportunities. By staying curious and attentive, you can detect subtle changes before they become significant forces of disruption.

Chapter 63: Apply Change as a Well-Designed Asset

Change is inevitable, but not all change is inherently beneficial. The key lies in applying change as a well-designed asset — a resource that you shape and direct toward achieving specific goals. When you actively harness change rather than reacting to it, you gain control over its outcomes and use it to create lasting value.

This mindset requires viewing change as an opportunity rather than a disruption. Instead of fearing uncertainty, ask how you can shape emerging trends, technologies, or challenges to benefit your goals. By proactively designing how you respond to change, you stay ahead of competitors and adapt to evolving circumstances with purpose.

Why Applying Change as an Asset is Effective

1. **Maximizes Opportunity:** Proactively shaping change turns potential disruptions into strategic advantages.

---

2. **Reduces Risk:** A structured approach to change minimizes negative impacts and improves outcomes.
3. **Encourages Innovation:** Using change creatively opens the door to new ideas and opportunities.

For example, businesses that reframe economic downturns as opportunities to streamline operations or diversify revenue streams often emerge stronger and more resilient.

How to Apply Change as an Asset

1. **Assess the Context:** Understand the nature of the change and its potential impact on your goals.
2. **Define Your Objective:** Decide how you want to leverage the change to achieve specific outcomes.
3. **Develop a Plan:** Create a step-by-step approach for integrating change into your strategy.
4. **Engage Your Team:** Involve others in brainstorming and implementing solutions, leveraging diverse perspectives.
5. **Monitor and Adjust:** Track progress and refine your approach as new developments unfold.

Real-World Example

In the early 2010s, Adidas used the rapid adoption of 3D printing as a strategic asset. While many companies hesitated to invest in the emerging technology, Adidas developed its Futurecraft line, featuring 3D-printed midsoles for its running shoes. By integrating change into its design process, Adidas created a product that combined innovation with functionality, boosting its reputation as a forward-thinking brand and attracting new customers.

Exercises

1. **Reframe a Current Challenge:** Identify a change you're facing and brainstorm ways to use it to your advantage.
2. **Create a Change Action Plan:** Choose one emerging trend and outline steps for incorporating it into your goals.
3. **Reflect on Past Success:** Think of a time when you successfully adapted to change. What lessons can you apply to future challenges?

Key Takeaway

Change becomes a powerful asset when you proactively shape and integrate it into your strategy. By approaching change as an opportunity for growth, you can transform challenges into valuable outcomes.

Chapter 64: Develop Options for Uncertain Futures

Uncertainty is a constant in any competitive environment, and the most successful individuals and organizations prepare by developing multiple options for the future. Rather than committing to a single path, they create flexibility, ensuring they can pivot as circumstances evolve. By building a portfolio of options, you mitigate risk, seize opportunities, and remain agile in the face of change.

This approach involves identifying key uncertainties, brainstorming potential scenarios, and preparing strategies for each. While it's impossible to predict the future with precision, creating options ensures you're ready to act no matter which direction the world takes.

Why Developing Options is Crucial

1. **Reduces Risk:** Multiple options provide fallback plans if initial strategies fail.

2. **Increases Agility:** Preparedness allows for quicker adaptation to unexpected changes.

3. **Encourages Confidence:** Knowing you have contingencies reduces stress and fosters decisive action.

For instance, organizations that diversify their supply chains are better equipped to handle disruptions such as political instability, natural disasters, or economic changes.

How to Develop Options for Uncertain Futures

1. **Identify Key Uncertainties:** Pinpoint the factors that could significantly impact your goals.

2. **Create Multiple Scenarios:** Envision different possible futures and how they might unfold.

3. **Develop Contingency Plans:** Prepare strategies and resources for each scenario.

4. **Test and Refine Options:** Pilot your strategies on a small scale to evaluate their feasibility.

5. **Remain Flexible:** Be willing to revise your options as new information emerges.

Real-World Example

During the early 2000s, Intel diversified its product offerings to prepare for shifts in the tech industry. Anticipating changes in demand for traditional computer processors, the company invested in technologies like mobile processors, server chips, and artificial intelligence. By developing multiple options, Intel remained a leader in a rapidly evolving market and positioned itself for long-term growth.

Exercises

1. **Brainstorm Future Scenarios:** Write down three possible futures that could impact your work or goals. What options could you prepare for each?

2. **Evaluate Your Current Options:** Are you overly reliant on a single strategy? Identify areas where diversification is needed.

3. **Test One Option:** Choose a potential strategy and implement it on a small scale to gauge its effectiveness.

Key Takeaway

Developing options for uncertain futures ensures you're ready to adapt, no matter what lies ahead. By preparing for multiple scenarios, you reduce risk and gain the confidence to navigate change with flexibility and foresight.

Chapter 65: Use Real Options to Hedge Strategies

OPPORTUNITIES

In strategic planning, uncertainty is unavoidable. One of the most effective ways to navigate it is by using real options—a framework that allows you to make flexible, staged decisions. Real options give you the ability to delay, expand, or abandon a course of action as new information becomes available, enabling you to hedge against risks while still pursuing opportunities.

Unlike traditional strategies that require a firm commitment upfront, real options recognize the value of flexibility. By keeping multiple paths open and making incremental investments, you maintain the ability to pivot without overcommitting. This approach is especially valuable in dynamic environments where the future is difficult to predict.

Why Real Options Are Powerful

1. **Minimizes Risk:** Real options reduce the cost of failure by allowing you to abandon unproductive paths early.

2. **Increases Agility:** Flexible strategies enable quick adjustments to changing circumstances.

3. **Encourages Exploration:** Small, initial investments lower the barrier to testing new ideas or markets.

For instance, a company considering international expansion might lease a small office or test a product in a single market before committing to full-scale operations.

How to Use Real Options

1. **Identify Opportunities:** Look for areas where flexibility could provide an advantage, such as emerging technologies or new markets.

2. **Break Down Decisions:** Divide your strategy into smaller, manageable steps with decision points along the way.

3. **Invest Incrementally:** Commit resources in stages, increasing investment only as conditions become clearer.

4. **Set Triggers for Action:** Define the conditions under which you'll expand, continue, or abandon a project.

5. **Evaluate Regularly:** Continuously assess the performance and feasibility of your options as circumstances evolve.

Real-World Example

Pharmaceutical companies often use real options in drug development. Instead of fully funding a drug from research to market, they start with smaller investments in early-stage trials. If the results are promising, they commit more resources to subsequent stages. This staged approach allows them to minimize losses if a drug fails while retaining the ability to capitalize on successful projects.

Exercises

1. **Create a Real Option:** Identify a decision you're currently facing and outline a plan to stage your commitments.

2. **Analyze a Past Decision:** Reflect on a situation where flexibility could have improved your outcome. How could real options have helped?

3. **Define Your Triggers:** Choose a current project and list the conditions that would prompt you to expand, pause, or abandon it.

Key Takeaway

Real options provide the flexibility to adapt your strategies to uncertainty. By staging decisions and committing incrementally, you reduce risk and maintain the agility to pivot as new opportunities or challenges arise.

Chapter 66: Develop Contingency Plans for Key Obstacles

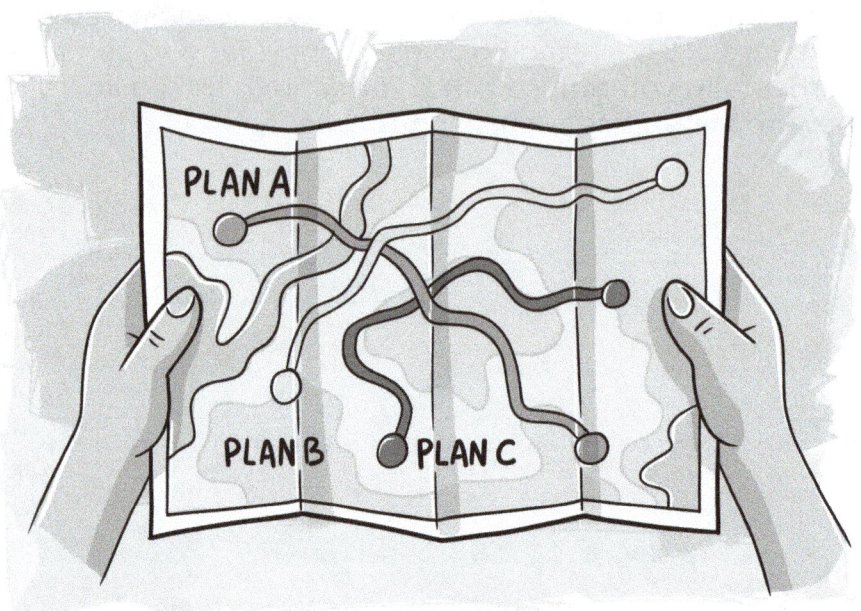

No strategy, no matter how well-designed, is immune to unexpected obstacles. Contingency plans ensure that you're prepared for setbacks by providing alternative actions when your primary plan encounters resistance. These plans act as a safety net, allowing you to continue progressing toward your goals even when challenges arise.

Developing effective contingency plans requires anticipating potential risks, assessing their likelihood, and preparing practical solutions. The process not only mitigates damage but also builds confidence, knowing that you're ready to respond effectively no matter what happens.

Why Contingency Plans Matter

1. **Reduces Disruption:** Quick responses minimize the impact of unexpected challenges.

2. **Increases Confidence:** Knowing you're prepared fosters calm and decisive action under pressure.

3. **Preserves Progress:** Contingency plans ensure that setbacks don't derail your overall strategy.

For example, organizations often prepare for cybersecurity breaches by developing incident response plans. These plans include steps for isolating the threat, securing data, and restoring systems, minimizing downtime and damage.

How to Develop Contingency Plans

1. **Identify Key Risks:** Analyze potential obstacles that could impact your goals or operations.
2. **Prioritize Risks:** Focus on the most likely and impactful challenges first.
3. **Define Alternative Actions:** Outline specific steps you'll take if a risk materializes.
4. **Allocate Resources:** Ensure that the necessary tools, personnel, or funds are available to implement your plan.
5. **Test and Revise Plans:** Conduct drills or simulations to assess your readiness and improve weak areas.

Real-World Example

In 2010, BP developed robust contingency plans following the Deepwater Horizon oil spill. Recognizing the risks associated with future offshore drilling, BP implemented advanced safety protocols, response drills, and new technologies to mitigate similar incidents.

One critical contingency was establishing partnerships with specialized environmental response teams to address spills rapidly if they occurred. This proactive planning not only reduced the likelihood of another disaster but also positioned BP as a company striving to rebuild trust through preparedness and accountability.

Exercises

1. **List Potential Obstacles:** Identify three risks that could impact your current goals. Outline contingency plans for each.
2. **Evaluate a Past Setback:** Think of a challenge you faced. How could a contingency plan have mitigated its impact?

3. **Test a Plan:** Choose one contingency plan and conduct a simulation or dry run to evaluate its effectiveness.

Key Takeaway

Contingency plans protect progress by preparing you for obstacles. By anticipating risks and defining clear alternative actions, you ensure resilience and adaptability in the face of unexpected challenges.

Chapter 67: Test Assumptions Before Acting

Assumptions are often the foundation of decisions, but when left untested, they can lead to costly mistakes. Testing assumptions before acting ensures that your strategies are based on accurate, validated information rather than guesswork. This process involves challenging preconceived notions, gathering evidence, and experimenting in low-risk environments to confirm that your assumptions hold true.

Whether you're launching a new product, entering a market, or implementing a change, assumptions play a crucial role in shaping your approach. By proactively questioning and validating these assumptions, you minimize risks and increase your chances of success.

Why Testing Assumptions Matters

1. **Reduces Risk:** Verifying assumptions minimizes the likelihood of failure by addressing potential flaws early.

2. **Informs Better Decisions:** Testing provides data-driven insights that improve the quality of your choices.

3. **Encourages Agility:** Identifying false assumptions allows you to pivot before fully committing resources.

For example, entrepreneurs often test assumptions about customer demand by launching minimum viable products (MVPs). These simplified versions of their offerings gauge market interest without significant investment, providing valuable feedback before scaling up.

How to Test Assumptions

1. **Identify Key Assumptions:** Pinpoint the beliefs or predictions that your strategy relies on most heavily.

2. **Design Small Experiments:** Develop low-risk tests to validate each assumption, such as surveys, prototypes, or pilot programs.

3. **Gather Evidence:** Collect data from real-world scenarios to confirm or disprove your assumptions.

4. **Iterate Based on Findings:** Use test results to refine your strategy, addressing weaknesses and building on strengths.

5. **Engage Stakeholders:** Involve your team or partners in testing to gain diverse perspectives and insights.

Real-World Example

Before opening its first store, Warby Parker tested the assumption that consumers would buy eyeglasses online. The founders launched a small-scale website, offering a limited number of frames to see if customers were willing to shop for eyewear without trying them on in person. The test was a success, proving that the concept resonated with consumers. This validation allowed Warby Parker to scale confidently, disrupting the eyewear industry.

Exercises

1. **List Your Assumptions:** Write down three assumptions underlying a current project or decision. How can you test them?

2. **Design a Small Experiment:** Create a low-cost, low-risk test to validate one of your assumptions this week.

3. **Evaluate Past Decisions:** Reflect on a decision where an untested assumption led to challenges. How could testing have improved the outcome?

Key Takeaway

Testing assumptions reduces risk and strengthens decisions by replacing guesswork with evidence. By validating your beliefs through small experiments, you ensure that your actions are based on reality, not speculation.

Chapter 68: Try Experimentation for Growth

Experimentation is the engine of growth. By testing new ideas, approaches, or strategies, you uncover opportunities that might otherwise remain hidden. Experimentation isn't about random trial and error—it's a structured process that involves setting hypotheses, testing in controlled environments, and analyzing results to learn what works.

In a rapidly changing world, businesses and individuals who embrace experimentation are better equipped to adapt and innovate. Experimentation not only drives growth but also fosters creativity, resilience, and a culture of continuous improvement.

Why Experimentation is Crucial for Growth

1. **Encourages Innovation:** Experiments reveal new possibilities and spark creative solutions.
2. **Reduces Uncertainty:** Testing ideas on a small scale minimizes risks before scaling up.

3. **Builds Resilience:** Experimentation fosters a mindset that views failure as a stepping stone to success.

For example, tech companies often use A/B testing to experiment with product features, website layouts, or marketing campaigns. By comparing results, they identify the most effective strategies for growth.

How to Try Experimentation for Growth

1. **Define Your Goals:** Clearly articulate what you want to achieve with your experiments.

2. **Set Hypotheses:** Develop predictions about what you expect to happen and why.

3. **Start Small:** Test ideas on a limited scale to minimize risks and costs.

4. **Measure Results:** Use data to evaluate the success of your experiments and identify areas for improvement.

5. **Iterate and Scale:** Refine your approach based on findings, scaling up successful experiments.

Real-World Example

Zappos embraced experimentation by offering a unique trial to test online shoe retailing. Founder Nick Swinmurn initially listed local shoe store inventories online and only purchased shoes once a customer placed an order. This experiment validated the concept without requiring a large upfront investment, paving the way for Zappos to revolutionize the e-commerce footwear industry.

Exercises

1. **Design an Experiment:** Identify one area where you could test a new idea. Outline your hypothesis, method, and measurement plan.

2. **Reflect on Past Experiments:** Think about a time when you tried something new. What worked, and what did you learn?

3. **Commit to a Growth Mindset:** Identify one risk or challenge you've avoided. How can experimentation help you address it?

Key Takeaway

Experimentation drives growth by uncovering new opportunities and fostering innovation. By testing ideas on a small scale, you minimize risks, learn from failures, and pave the way for success.

Chapter 69: Turn Failures into Stepping Stones for Progress

Failure is an inevitable part of innovation and growth, but its impact depends entirely on how you respond to it. Viewing failures as stepping stones rather than dead ends transforms setbacks into valuable learning opportunities. By analyzing what went wrong, you gain insights that refine your strategies, improve decision-making, and prepare you for future challenges.

Turning failures into progress requires a shift in mindset. Rather than focusing on the negative aspects of a setback, consider what it has taught you and how it can shape your next steps. This approach not only builds resilience but also encourages a culture where experimentation and risk-taking are embraced as necessary for long-term success.

Why Learning from Failure is Crucial

1. **Fosters Growth:** Each failure provides unique lessons that refine your skills and strategies.

2. **Builds Resilience:** Overcoming setbacks strengthens your ability to adapt to future challenges.

3. **Encourages Innovation:** When failure is seen as a learning opportunity, it inspires bold, creative approaches.

For example, failure often drives breakthroughs in scientific research. Many important discoveries, from penicillin to post-it notes, began as unintentional outcomes of experiments. By analyzing "failures," researchers uncovered ground-breaking innovations.

How to Turn Failures into Progress

1. **Reflect and Analyze:** Take time to understand what went wrong and why. Break down the failure into specific elements to identify areas for improvement.

2. **Extract Lessons:** Write down the key insights you've gained from the setback and how they can inform your future actions.

3. **Reframe Your Mindset:** View failure as part of the process rather than an endpoint. Celebrate the courage it took to take a risk.

4. **Share Learnings:** If you're part of a team, openly discuss what happened to foster a culture of learning and transparency.

5. **Apply the Lessons:** Use what you've learned to refine your approach and take smarter risks moving forward.

Real-World Example

The video game company Rovio, the creators of *Angry Birds*, failed with over 50 game releases before achieving massive success. Each failed game provided insights into what resonated with players, helping Rovio refine its design and marketing strategies. The eventual launch of *Angry Birds* turned the company into a global sensation, proving the value of persistence and learning from failure.

Exercises

1. **Reflect on a Failure:** Identify a recent setback. Write down what caused it and three lessons you can take from it.

2. **Redesign Your Approach:** Based on the lessons from a past failure, outline a new strategy to address a similar challenge.

3. **Encourage Failure Discussions:** If you're part of a team, create a safe space for discussing mistakes and the insights gained from them.

Key Takeaway

Failure isn't the end; it's a stepping stone to success. By learning from setbacks and applying those lessons, you transform obstacles into opportunities for growth and innovation.

Chapter 70: Adapt Plans in Real Time

Even the most well-thought-out plans can be disrupted by unexpected changes. The ability to adapt plans in real time ensures that you remain flexible and responsive, allowing you to navigate challenges and seize opportunities as they arise. This adaptability is a hallmark of resilient individuals and organizations, turning potential setbacks into stepping stones for success.

Real-time adaptation involves constantly monitoring the situation, identifying when a shift is necessary, and making quick, informed adjustments. It's not about abandoning your overall goals but about finding alternative paths to achieve them when the original plan no longer fits the circumstances.

Why Real-Time Adaptation is Vital

1. **Maintains Momentum:** Quick adjustments keep progress moving forward despite obstacles.

2. **Seizes Opportunities:** Staying flexible allows you to capitalize on unexpected advantages.

3. **Reduces Stress:** Having a mindset of adaptability lessens the pressure of rigidly adhering to a failing plan.

For example, adapting a marketing campaign based on real-time customer feedback can transform mediocre results into success. When Nike launched its "You Can't Stop Us" campaign during the COVID-19 pandemic, it pivoted to emphasize unity and resilience, resonating deeply with global audiences.

How to Adapt Plans in Real Time

1. **Stay Informed:** Continuously monitor progress and changes in the environment that could impact your plans.

2. **Foster Flexibility:** Build plans with room for adjustment, such as buffer time or modular strategies.

3. **Define Core Goals:** Keep your end objectives clear so you can adapt methods without losing focus.

4. **Involve Your Team:** Collaborate with others to brainstorm solutions and identify the best path forward.

5. **Act Decisively:** Avoid paralysis by analysis—make adjustments quickly based on available information.

Real-World Example

The 2021 Tokyo Olympics showcased real-time adaptability when faced with the COVID-19 pandemic. Organizers adjusted protocols, postponed events, and implemented health measures to ensure the games could proceed safely. These rapid adaptations allowed the event to succeed despite unprecedented challenges.

Exercises

1. **Review a Recent Change:** Think of a time when you had to pivot quickly. What worked well, and what could you improve?

2. **Practice Scenario Planning:** Identify a current project and outline two potential disruptions. How would you adapt?

3. **Build Flexibility:** Analyze a current plan and identify areas where you can introduce more adaptability.

Key Takeaway

Adapting plans in real time ensures resilience and responsiveness in the face of change. By staying informed and flexible, you maintain progress and turn unexpected challenges into opportunities for success.

Chapter 71: Detect Hidden Patterns in Chaos

Chaos often feels overwhelming, but beneath the surface lies hidden order waiting to be uncovered. Detecting patterns in chaos is a critical adaptive strategy that enables you to make sense of complexity, anticipate future outcomes, and act decisively in uncertain environments. The ability to see connections where others see randomness is what separates reactive individuals from strategic thinkers.

Finding patterns doesn't require special foresight — it demands focus, curiosity, and a willingness to examine situations from multiple perspectives. By identifying recurring themes, trends, or relationships, you gain insights that guide smarter decisions and innovative solutions.

Why Detecting Patterns in Chaos is Valuable

1. **Reveals Insights:** Identifying patterns helps you understand the underlying factors driving events.

2. **Improves Decision-Making:** Recognizing order in complexity enables faster, more confident choices.

3. **Enhances Predictability:** Patterns provide clues about what might happen next, allowing you to stay ahead.

For example, stock market analysts often look for patterns in trading data to predict price movements. While the market can seem chaotic, these patterns offer valuable insights for strategic investment decisions.

How to Detect Hidden Patterns in Chaos

1. **Zoom Out:** Step back from the details to view the bigger picture, which often reveals broader trends.

2. **Focus on Key Variables:** Identify the most important factors influencing the situation and track their interactions.

3. **Use Data and Analytics:** Leverage tools and methods that help you visualize complex information, such as charts or heatmaps.

4. **Engage Diverse Perspectives:** Collaborate with others who can offer different viewpoints, uncovering connections you might miss.

5. **Test Your Observations:** Validate potential patterns by checking their consistency across different scenarios.

Real-World Example

The British cryptanalysts at Bletchley Park during World War II famously detected hidden patterns in the seemingly chaotic messages encrypted by the German Enigma machine. By identifying recurring structures and analyzing vast amounts of intercepted data, they broke the code, providing crucial intelligence that helped win the war.

Exercises

1. **Identify a Chaotic Situation:** Reflect on a current challenge that feels disorganized. Write down potential patterns or recurring elements you notice.

2. **Analyze Data for Trends:** Choose a set of data (e.g., sales, performance metrics, or feedback) and look for correlations or trends.

3. **Collaborate for Insight:** Discuss a complex problem with a colleague or friend to explore new patterns you may not have considered.

Key Takeaway

Detecting hidden patterns in chaos transforms uncertainty into opportunity. By focusing on connections and recurring themes, you uncover the insights needed to act strategically in complex environments.

Chapter 72: Use Contrarian Thinking to Your Advantage

Contrarian thinking involves questioning popular beliefs and exploring alternative perspectives. While conventional wisdom often has merit, blindly following it can lead to missed opportunities and vulnerabilities. Contrarian thinkers challenge assumptions, evaluate evidence critically, and identify overlooked possibilities, giving them a strategic edge.

This approach doesn't mean opposing the majority for its own sake. Instead, it requires disciplined analysis to determine when a different path might yield better results. In a world where many follow trends, contrarian thinkers are often the first to spot flaws, inefficiencies, or untapped opportunities.

Why Contrarian Thinking is Powerful

1. **Exposes Weaknesses:** Challenging the status quo reveals blind spots or overlooked risks.

2. **Uncovers Opportunities:** Alternative perspectives often highlight paths others ignore.

3. **Drives Innovation:** Thinking differently fosters creative solutions and unique strategies.

For example, contrarian thinking allowed Howard Schultz to transform Starbucks from a small coffee shop into a global brand. At a time when coffee was seen as a utilitarian product, Schultz envisioned coffee as an experience. By challenging the industry's norms, he created a new market and redefined how people consume coffee.

How to Use Contrarian Thinking

1. **Question Assumptions:** Regularly challenge conventional beliefs, especially those that drive important decisions.

2. **Explore Opposing Views:** Seek out perspectives that contradict your own to identify potential gaps in your thinking.

3. **Analyze Underlying Evidence:** Focus on data rather than opinions when evaluating popular trends.

4. **Test Your Ideas:** Pilot contrarian approaches on a small scale before committing fully.

5. **Stay Open-Minded:** Balance doubt with curiosity, remaining open to learning and adapting.

Real-World Example

In the late 1990s, Reed Hastings, co-founder of Netflix, applied contrarian thinking by launching a subscription-based DVD rental service at a time when video rental stores dominated. His approach challenged the traditional model of renting movies by eliminating late fees and offering convenience. This disruption ultimately led to Netflix's rise as a market leader, while competitors like Blockbuster failed to adapt.

Exercises

1. **Challenge a Norm:** Identify one commonly held belief in your industry or field. Ask yourself: What if the opposite were true?

2. **Seek Contrarian Opinions:** Talk to someone with a different viewpoint on a key issue. What insights can you gain?

3. **Pilot a Contrarian Idea:** Test an unconventional strategy or approach in a low-risk scenario.

Key Takeaway

Contrarian thinking reveals opportunities hidden in plain sight. By questioning assumptions and exploring alternative perspectives, you position yourself to innovate and succeed where others follow the crowd.

Chapter 73: Stay Agile in Dynamic Environments

Agility is the ability to respond quickly and effectively to changing circumstances, making it an essential strategy in dynamic environments. Whether you're navigating shifting market trends, technological advancements, or unexpected disruptions, staying agile allows you to adapt and thrive.

Being agile doesn't mean abandoning long-term planning — it means integrating flexibility into your strategy so you can pivot without losing sight of your goals. Agility is about maintaining momentum, fostering innovation, and embracing change as an opportunity rather than a threat.

Why Agility is Crucial in Dynamic Environments

1. **Enables Rapid Response:** Agility allows you to act quickly when circumstances change, reducing the impact of challenges.

2. **Encourages Innovation:** Flexible strategies foster creative solutions to new problems.

3. **Builds Resilience:** Organizations and individuals who stay agile are better equipped to handle uncertainty and bounce back from setbacks.

For example, businesses that embraced remote work technologies early were able to maintain productivity during times of disruption. Agility in adopting new tools allowed them to minimize downtime and sustain operations.

How to Stay Agile

1. **Embrace a Growth Mindset:** View change as an opportunity to learn and improve rather than a threat.
2. **Streamline Decision-Making:** Reduce bureaucratic barriers to enable quick, effective decisions.
3. **Monitor the Environment:** Stay informed about trends and developments that could impact your goals.
4. **Encourage Collaboration:** Build teams that communicate openly and adapt collectively to challenges.
5. **Test and Iterate:** Regularly review and refine your strategies to ensure they remain relevant.

Real-World Example

In the 2010s, T-Mobile disrupted the rigid telecommunications industry by adopting an agile, customer-first approach. The company launched its "Un-carrier" strategy, eliminating contracts, offering unlimited data plans, and providing free international roaming.

While competitors clung to traditional practices like restrictive contracts and hidden fees, T-Mobile's agility allowed it to quickly address customer frustrations and attract millions of new subscribers. By staying flexible and responsive to consumer needs, T-Mobile transformed itself into a major player in the U.S. mobile market.

Exercises

1. **Identify a Change:** Reflect on a recent shift in your industry or environment. How could agility help you respond effectively?

2. **Streamline a Process:** Choose one area of your work where decision-making could be faster or more flexible. Implement a change this week.

3. **Embrace Feedback:** Solicit input from others about how you can become more adaptable in your current role or projects.

Key Takeaway

Agility is the key to thriving in dynamic environments. By staying flexible, informed, and innovative, you turn challenges into opportunities and maintain momentum in the face of change.

Chapter 74: Exploit Adversaries' Rigidity

Rigidity can be a significant weakness. Adversaries who cling to fixed strategies or resist change often leave themselves vulnerable to those who can adapt and innovate. By exploiting this rigidity, you gain an edge, outmaneuvering competitors who fail to recognize the need for flexibility.

Exploiting rigidity doesn't mean acting unethically; it's about understanding your adversaries' limitations and capitalizing on their inability to adjust. Whether in business, sports, or negotiation, recognizing and leveraging rigidity allows you to turn their predictability into your advantage.

Why Exploiting Rigidity Works

1. **Creates Opportunities:** Predictable behavior makes adversaries easier to anticipate and counter.
2. **Highlights Your Strengths:** Flexibility and creativity become powerful tools when others lack them.

3. **Drives Competitive Advantage:** Capitalizing on rigidity ensures you stay one step ahead in dynamic situations.

For instance, Blockbuster's reluctance to adapt to the rise of digital streaming was exploited by emerging companies like Hulu and Amazon Prime Video. While Blockbuster stuck to its physical rental store model, these agile competitors embraced the streaming revolution, offering consumers convenience and on-demand access to entertainment.

By the time Blockbuster attempted to adjust, its rigid approach had allowed competitors to dominate the market, leaving little room for recovery.

How to Exploit Adversaries' Rigidity

1. **Analyze Their Patterns:** Study competitors' strategies and identify areas where they're resistant to change.
2. **Anticipate Their Moves:** Use their predictability to plan counterstrategies and stay ahead.
3. **Leverage Innovation:** Introduce new ideas or approaches that disrupt their fixed methods.
4. **Create Pressure Points:** Force them into situations where their rigidity becomes a disadvantage.
5. **Stay Adaptive:** Ensure your strategies remain flexible to maintain your advantage.

Real-World Example

In the early 2000s, Salesforce disrupted the enterprise software industry by offering customer relationship management (CRM) tools through a cloud-based subscription model. Traditional software providers, like Oracle and SAP, relied on rigid, on-premises installations with high upfront costs.

By exploiting these companies' reluctance to embrace cloud technology, Salesforce captured a growing market of businesses seeking flexible, cost-effective solutions. This approach not only redefined how software was delivered but also established Salesforce as a dominant force in the tech industry.

Exercises

1. **Identify Rigidity:** Think of a competitor or challenge where rigidity is evident. How could you capitalize on it?
2. **Challenge Predictability:** Examine your own strategies. Are there areas where you've become too rigid?
3. **Develop a Disruptive Idea:** Brainstorm an innovative approach that could disrupt the status quo in your field.

Key Takeaway

Exploiting adversaries' rigidity gives you a strategic advantage. By recognizing their limitations and staying adaptive, you turn their predictability into opportunities for innovation and success.

Chapter 75: Be Unpredictable to Stay Ahead

Predictability is a liability in competitive environments. When adversaries can easily anticipate your next move, they can counter your strategies and neutralize your efforts. Being unpredictable forces others to stay reactive, giving you the upper hand by keeping them guessing.

Unpredictability isn't about chaos or randomness — it's about introducing elements of surprise and variety in your actions while maintaining alignment with your goals. This strategic use of unpredictability allows you to gain the element of surprise, disrupt your adversaries' plans, and remain ahead of the competition.

Why Being Unpredictable is Effective

1. **Keeps Adversaries Reactive:** Opponents can't plan effectively when they're unsure of your next move.

2. **Creates Opportunities:** Surprise maneuvers open new paths that others didn't anticipate.

3. **Establishes a Psychological Edge:** Unpredictability creates doubt and hesitation in adversaries, giving you the advantage.

For instance, in negotiations, changing your approach mid-discussion — such as pivoting to a new offer or using an unexpected tone — can shift the dynamic in your favor.

How to Be Unpredictable Strategically

1. **Break Patterns:** Avoid falling into repetitive routines or habits that others can easily recognize.
2. **Introduce Variability:** Rotate strategies, tactics, or approaches to maintain an element of surprise.
3. **Combine Predictable with Unpredictable Actions:** Create a baseline of reliability to build trust, but occasionally introduce unexpected moves to disrupt expectations.
4. **Monitor Reactions:** Pay attention to how others respond to your unpredictability and adjust accordingly.
5. **Stay True to Your Goals:** Ensure that your unpredictability aligns with your broader objectives and doesn't create unnecessary confusion.

Real-World Example

Ryanair, the low-cost airline, demonstrated unpredictability in its pricing strategies. Unlike traditional airlines, which maintained fixed pricing structures, Ryanair implemented dynamic pricing that adjusted based on demand, competitor actions, and even time of day. This unpredictability left competitors scrambling to match fares, while Ryanair consistently attracted cost-conscious travelers and maximized revenue.

Exercises

1. **Identify a Routine:** Find a predictable pattern in your actions or strategies. How can you introduce an element of surprise?
2. **Test an Unpredictable Move:** In a current project or negotiation, try an unexpected approach and observe the reaction.

3. **Analyze an Adversary's Predictability:** Look for predictable patterns in a competitor's behavior. How could you disrupt their expectations?

Key Takeaway

Strategic unpredictability keeps you ahead by disrupting expectations and forcing others to stay reactive. By introducing surprise in your actions, you gain the psychological and competitive edge needed to succeed.

Chapter 76: Diversify Your Cheat Sheet

Relying on a single strategy or skillset can leave you vulnerable when circumstances change. Diversifying your "cheat sheet" ensures that you're prepared for a variety of challenges, allowing you to respond effectively in any situation. Whether you're navigating a competitive market, solving complex problems, or seizing new opportunities, having a diverse toolkit gives you flexibility and resilience.

Diversification involves expanding your knowledge, skills, and resources to create a broad foundation for success. It's not about being a jack-of-all-trades but about having enough options to adapt your approach when needed. By doing so, you reduce dependency on any one tactic and increase your chances of achieving your goals.

Why Diversifying is Crucial

1. **Increases Flexibility:** A broader toolkit allows you to pivot when a single approach fails.

2. **Mitigates Risk:** Diversification minimizes the impact of setbacks in any one area.

3. **Encourages Growth:** Learning new skills and strategies keeps you adaptable and innovative.

For example, financial investors diversify their portfolios by spreading assets across stocks, bonds, and other instruments to reduce risk and improve returns. Similarly, strategic thinkers can diversify their approaches to remain resilient in unpredictable environments.

How to Diversify Your Cheat Sheet

1. **Learn Continuously:** Commit to expanding your knowledge and skills in areas relevant to your goals.

2. **Experiment with New Approaches:** Test different strategies and tactics to see what works in various contexts.

3. **Build a Diverse Network:** Surround yourself with people from different industries, backgrounds, and expertise to gain fresh perspectives.

4. **Create Backup Plans:** Develop alternative strategies to ensure you're prepared for unexpected challenges.

5. **Embrace Flexibility:** Stay open to change and ready to pivot when needed.

Real-World Example

Disney exemplifies diversification through its business model. While initially focused on animated films, Disney expanded into theme parks, merchandise, television, and streaming services. This diverse "cheat sheet" allowed the company to weather industry disruptions and remain a global leader in entertainment.

Exercises

1. **Assess Your Toolkit:** Identify your current skills, resources, and strategies. What's missing that could strengthen your adaptability?

2. **Try Something New:** Choose one area where you lack experience and take a small step to expand your knowledge or skills.

3. **Build a Diverse Plan:** Create a strategy that includes at least three different approaches to achieving a single goal.

Key Takeaway

Diversifying your cheat sheet ensures you're ready for any challenge. By expanding your skills, strategies, and resources, you create a flexible foundation for sustained success.

Chapter 77: Counterpoise Risk and Reward Over Time

Every strategic decision involves some degree of risk and reward. The art of counterpoising — or balancing — these factors over time ensures that you make calculated moves that align with your long-term goals. Risk and reward are not static; they shift as circumstances evolve. Successful individuals and organizations are those who continuously reassess these factors and adjust their strategies accordingly.

Counterpoising risk and reward isn't about eliminating risk entirely—some degree of risk is necessary for growth. Instead, it's about understanding the relationship between the two and making decisions that maximize potential benefits while keeping risks manageable. By viewing risk and reward as interconnected forces, you can navigate uncertainty with confidence and precision.

Why Counterpoising Risk and Reward is Critical

1. **Mitigates Overexposure:** Balancing ensures that risks don't outweigh potential rewards, protecting you from unnecessary losses.
2. **Optimizes Opportunities:** Careful evaluation helps you seize high-reward opportunities without recklessness.
3. **Builds Long-Term Resilience:** Sustainable decisions prevent burnout or resource depletion over time.

For example, investors often use diversification to balance risk and reward. By spreading investments across different asset classes, they reduce the impact of losses in any one area while still pursuing growth opportunities.

How to Counterpoise Risk and Reward

1. **Assess the Stakes:** Evaluate the potential risks and rewards of a decision in both the short and long term.
2. **Start Small:** Test high-risk strategies on a smaller scale to minimize potential losses.
3. **Monitor Continuously:** Regularly review how your decisions are performing and adjust as needed.
4. **Diversify Your Approach:** Spread risks across multiple strategies to avoid overdependence on a single outcome.
5. **Know Your Threshold:** Understand your risk tolerance and set clear limits to avoid overcommitting.

Real-World Example

SpaceX exemplifies this principle in its approach to innovation. While the company takes significant risks in developing reusable rockets, it balances these risks with incremental testing. For example, prototypes like Starship undergo multiple test flights to identify flaws and reduce risk before full-scale deployment. This method allows SpaceX to pursue ground-breaking innovations while minimizing catastrophic failures.

Exercises

1. **Evaluate a Current Decision:** Write down the risks and rewards of a choice you're facing. How can you adjust your approach to achieve a better balance?

2. **Create a Risk-Reward Matrix:** Categorize potential decisions into high-risk/high-reward, low-risk/low-reward, and other combinations to identify your best options.

3. **Set a Risk Limit:** Define a clear boundary for the level of risk you're willing to accept in your current projects.

Key Takeaway

Counterpoising risk and reward over time ensures sustainable success. By continually evaluating and balancing these factors, you make informed decisions that maximize benefits while protecting yourself from unnecessary losses.

Chapter 78: Thrive in Nonlinear Scenarios

Life rarely unfolds in a straight line. Nonlinear scenarios are those where outcomes are unpredictable, relationships between actions and results are complex, and progress feels anything but linear. Thriving in such situations requires the ability to adapt, embrace uncertainty, and find creative solutions that align with your broader objectives.

Nonlinear scenarios demand flexibility and resilience. Instead of rigidly following a predefined plan, you must recognize patterns, pivot when necessary, and trust that even small actions can lead to significant breakthroughs. By focusing on adaptability rather than control, you can navigate nonlinear challenges effectively.

Why Thriving in Nonlinear Scenarios is Important

1. **Encourages Innovation:** Complexity often opens the door to new ideas and solutions.

2. **Builds Resilience:** Embracing unpredictability strengthens your ability to handle uncertainty.

3. **Fosters Long-Term Success:** Adaptability ensures progress even when the path is unclear.

For instance, entrepreneurs often encounter nonlinear growth. Early progress may seem slow or unpredictable, but persistence and adaptation often lead to exponential success as markets mature and opportunities align.

How to Thrive in Nonlinear Scenarios

1. **Embrace Complexity:** Accept that outcomes may not follow a direct path, and remain open to unexpected results.

2. **Focus on Core Goals:** Keep your overarching objectives in mind, even as you adapt your methods.

3. **Experiment Strategically:** Test multiple approaches to find what works in a complex environment.

4. **Re-evaluate Regularly:** Continuously assess your progress and adjust your strategies as needed.

5. **Celebrate Small Wins:** Recognize incremental progress as a sign that you're moving in the right direction.

Real-World Example

The development of CRISPR gene-editing technology highlights thriving in nonlinear scenarios. Early research in bacterial defense mechanisms led to the discovery of a revolutionary tool for editing DNA. The path to this breakthrough was not linear — it involved years of trial and error, unexpected findings, and collaboration across disciplines. Today, CRISPR is transforming medicine, agriculture, and biotechnology.

Exercises

1. **Identify a Nonlinear Challenge:** Reflect on a situation where progress has been unpredictable. How can you adjust your approach to better navigate it?

2. **Experiment with New Approaches:** Brainstorm three alternative methods to tackle a current complex problem.

---

3. **Celebrate Incremental Wins:** Write down three small successes from a nonlinear project and how they contribute to your long-term goals.

Key Takeaway

Thriving in nonlinear scenarios requires adaptability, creativity, and a focus on long-term objectives. By embracing complexity and adjusting your approach, you turn unpredictability into a source of innovation and growth.

Chapter 79: Prepare for Worst-Case Scenarios

Hope for the best, but always prepare for the worst. This classic principle is essential in any adaptive strategy. Worst-case scenarios, though unpleasant to imagine, can devastate unprepared individuals, teams, or organizations. Preparation is not about pessimism — it's about resilience. When you've planned for the most challenging outcomes, you can approach uncertainty with confidence, knowing that even the most significant disruptions won't derail you entirely.

Worst-case scenario planning doesn't mean focusing exclusively on negative outcomes. Instead, it's about identifying potential risks, understanding their impact, and creating robust systems to mitigate them. By preparing for the unexpected, you create a safety net that allows you to respond effectively, protect your interests, and even find opportunities within the chaos.

Why Preparing for the Worst is Crucial

1. **Reduces Panic:** Knowing you have a plan in place minimizes stress during a crisis.

2. **Ensures Continuity:** Preparation keeps operations running, even in difficult conditions.

3. **Builds Confidence:** When the worst is accounted for, you can focus on achieving your goals.

For example, many tech companies prepare for cyberattacks by investing in robust cybersecurity systems and developing incident response plans. This proactive approach reduces downtime and protects valuable data when attacks occur.

How to Prepare for Worst-Case Scenarios

1. **Identify Risks:** Assess potential threats to your goals, such as economic downturns, operational failures, or market shifts.

2. **Assess Impact:** Determine the likelihood and severity of each risk to prioritize your planning.

3. **Develop Mitigation Plans:** Create specific actions to reduce the probability or impact of each worst-case scenario.

4. **Stockpile Resources:** Ensure you have the tools, funds, or networks needed to respond effectively.

5. **Practice Your Plans:** Run simulations or drills to identify gaps in your preparation and refine your strategies.

Real-World Example

In the aviation industry, pilots and airlines meticulously prepare for worst-case scenarios, such as engine failures or extreme weather conditions. Training programs, redundant systems, and clear protocols ensure that even in the most challenging situations, pilots can respond effectively and prioritize passenger safety. This rigorous preparation is why air travel remains one of the safest modes of transportation.

Exercises

1. **List Your Risks:** Write down three worst-case scenarios that could impact your work or goals. Outline potential responses for each.

2. **Test a Plan:** Conduct a simulation of one of your worst-case scenarios to evaluate your readiness.

3. **Build Resilience:** Identify one area where you lack contingency measures and take steps to address it.

Key Takeaway

Preparing for worst-case scenarios builds resilience and ensures you're ready for anything. By anticipating challenges and developing strong contingency plans, you protect your goals and maintain confidence in uncertain times.

Chapter 80: Apply the OODA Loop: Observe, Orient, Decide, Act

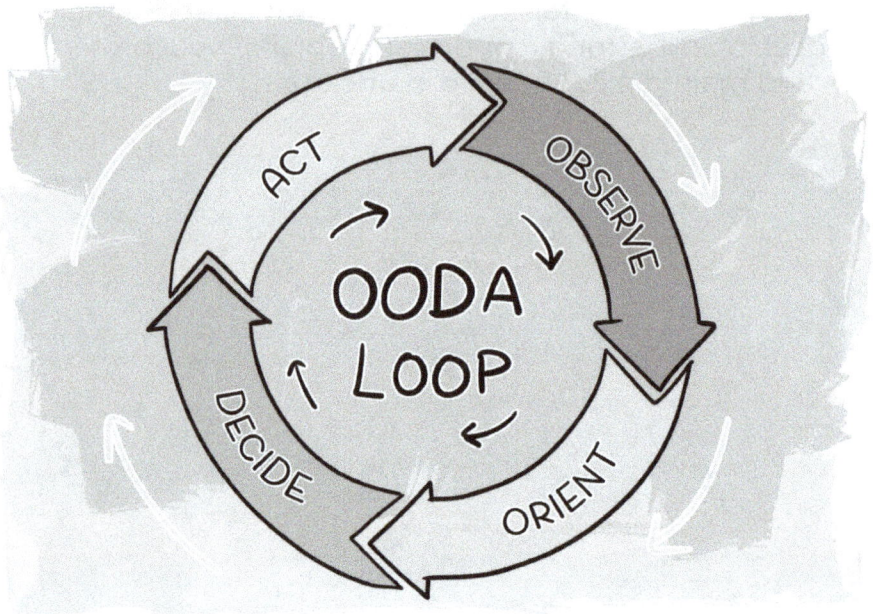

The OODA loop, developed by military strategist John Boyd, is a powerful decision-making framework that emphasizes speed, adaptability, and continuous improvement. The four steps — Observe, Orient, Decide, and Act — allow you to navigate complex situations effectively, respond to change swiftly, and stay ahead of the competition.

The OODA loop is particularly valuable in dynamic environments where circumstances evolve rapidly. It encourages you to gather information, analyze your position, make a decision, and take action — all while remaining flexible and ready to adjust as new developments arise. This iterative process ensures that you don't get stuck in analysis paralysis or fall behind due to slow responses.

The Four Steps of the OODA Loop

1. **Observe:** Gather information about your environment, competitors, and any changes affecting your situation. The goal is to develop a clear understanding of what's happening around you.

2. **Orient:** Analyze the information you've gathered, assess your position, and determine the opportunities or threats you face. This step involves synthesizing data and aligning it with your goals.

3. **Decide:** Based on your analysis, choose a course of action. Speed is critical here—delaying decisions gives others the opportunity to act first.

4. **Act:** Implement your decision decisively while remaining prepared to adapt if the situation changes.

Why the OODA Loop is Effective

1. **Increases Agility:** The loop's iterative nature ensures you can adapt to new developments quickly.

2. **Improves Decision-Making:** Breaking decisions into manageable steps reduces complexity and boosts confidence.

3. **Keeps You Ahead:** Rapid observation and action allow you to outpace competitors or adversaries.

Real-World Example

Amazon effectively applies the OODA loop in its approach to customer experience. The company continually observes customer behaviors through data, orients itself by analyzing trends, decides on improvements, and acts quickly to implement them. For example, the introduction of one-click ordering and same-day delivery demonstrates Amazon's ability to respond rapidly to evolving customer expectations, keeping it ahead in the e-commerce space.

How to Apply the OODA Loop

1. **Start Small:** Practice the OODA loop on smaller decisions to build confidence and efficiency.

2. **Stay Alert:** Continuously monitor your environment to stay informed about changes.

3. **Be Decisive:** Prioritize speed without sacrificing accuracy in your decision-making.

4. **Evaluate Outcomes:** After acting, analyze the results and refine your approach for the next iteration.

Exercises

1. **Apply the OODA Loop:** Choose a current challenge and walk through each step—Observe, Orient, Decide, Act—to address it.

2. **Evaluate a Past Decision:** Reflect on a situation where applying the OODA loop could have improved your response.

3. **Practice Rapid Decisions:** Set a timer and work through the OODA loop to solve a low-stakes problem quickly.

Key Takeaway

The OODA loop is a powerful framework for navigating dynamic environments. By observing, orienting, deciding, and acting in an iterative process, you stay agile, responsive, and ahead of the competition.

Part 5: Advanced Strategies

This final section is where everything converges. Now that the foundations, tactical executions, and long-term planning are in place, you're ready to operate at the systems level. These chapters will help you manage intricate trade-offs, anticipate ripple effects, and engineer strategies that self-reinforce over time. Part 5 explores the nuance of timing, authority, group dynamics, and predictive modeling — giving you tools not just to compete, but to control the terrain.

Chapter 81: Orchestrate Complex Systems for Advantage

In today's interconnected world, success often depends on your ability to orchestrate complex systems effectively. Whether managing a supply chain, coordinating a team, or navigating market dynamics, you're dealing with intricate networks of moving parts that must work together seamlessly. The key to thriving in such environments lies in orchestrating these components in a way that amplifies their collective value.

Complex systems are dynamic, meaning that small adjustments in one area can ripple across the entire structure. Your job as a strategist is to harmonize these interactions, ensuring they align with your overarching objectives. It's not about controlling every detail—it's about creating a structure where each part functions optimally while contributing to the whole.

Why Orchestrating Complex Systems is Critical

1. **Unlocks Synergy:** When the elements of a system align, their combined impact exceeds the sum of their parts.
2. **Enhances Adaptability:** A well-orchestrated system can quickly adjust to changes without losing efficiency.
3. **Maximizes Efficiency:** Streamlining interactions reduces friction, redundancies, and wasted resources.

For example, in urban planning, city governments must balance housing, transportation, public services, and environmental sustainability. By managing these interconnected elements strategically, they create cities that are livable, resilient, and efficient.

How to Orchestrate Complex Systems

1. **Visualize the System:** Map out all components and their relationships. Understanding the system as a whole is the first step to managing it effectively.
2. **Define Key Objectives:** Set clear, overarching goals that guide the system's operation.
3. **Optimize Interactions:** Look for inefficiencies in how components work together and address them.
4. **Leverage Technology:** Use tools like analytics software, dashboards, or automation to monitor and manage complexity.
5. **Adapt Continuously:** Be prepared to adjust your system as external conditions or internal needs evolve.

Real-World Example

In Formula 1 racing, teams like Mercedes excel at orchestrating complex systems. A race car's performance relies on seamless collaboration between engineers, mechanics, strategists, and drivers. Each team member focuses on their specialized role, while advanced data analytics monitor every aspect of the car's performance in real time. By aligning these diverse elements, Formula 1 teams consistently deliver precision, speed, and reliability.

Exercises

1. **Map Your System:** Identify the key components of a system you're managing and visualize how they interact.

2. **Spot Weak Links:** Analyze one area where inefficiencies or misalignments exist. How can you improve it?

3. **Set a System-Wide Goal:** Define an objective that unites all elements of your system, and ensure each part contributes toward it.

Key Takeaway

Orchestrating complex systems turns challenges into opportunities. By aligning interconnected components toward a shared goal, you create synergy, efficiency, and sustained success.

Chapter 82: Manage Trade-Offs with Precision

Every decision comes with trade-offs—choosing one path means sacrificing another. Successful strategists recognize that trade-offs aren't obstacles; they're opportunities to clarify priorities and focus resources where they'll create the most value. Managing trade-offs with precision ensures that every choice serves your larger goals, even if it requires difficult sacrifices.

Trade-offs arise in various forms: speed versus quality, individual needs versus team objectives, or short-term gains versus long-term stability. Rather than avoiding trade-offs, embrace them as part of the decision-making process. A precise approach means weighing options carefully, communicating openly, and aligning choices with your strategic vision.

Why Managing Trade-Offs is Essential

1. **Clarifies Priorities:** Deliberate trade-offs force you to focus on what truly matters.

2. **Maximizes Impact:** Allocating resources wisely ensures you achieve the greatest returns.

3. **Prevents Burnout:** Recognizing limits avoids overextending yourself or your team.

For instance, when companies expand into new markets, they often face the trade-off between rapid growth and maintaining operational quality. The best expansions balance these priorities, scaling at a sustainable pace without sacrificing their core values.

How to Manage Trade-Offs

1. **Define Your Objectives:** Start by clarifying the results you want to achieve. Let these guide your decisions.

2. **Weigh Costs and Benefits:** Analyze the impact of each option to determine which aligns best with your goals.

3. **Communicate Transparently:** Share your reasoning with stakeholders to build trust and alignment.

4. **Review Regularly:** Reevaluate your choices to ensure they remain effective as circumstances change.

5. **Be Willing to Pivot:** If new information arises, don't hesitate to adjust your approach.

Real-World Example

In the 1990s, Procter & Gamble (P&G) faced a trade-off when deciding how to allocate resources between its established product lines and its emerging Swiffer brand. The company realized that focusing too heavily on legacy products could hinder innovation, but diverting too many resources to Swiffer could disrupt its existing market dominance.

P&G managed this trade-off by incrementally investing in Swiffer while leveraging its existing distribution and marketing channels to support the new product. This approach allowed P&G to maintain the strength of its established brands while introducing a groundbreaking product that became a billion-dollar success. The Swiffer's eventual dominance in the cleaning category highlights the precision with which P&G managed competing priorities.

Exercises

1. **Identify a Current Trade-Off:** Think of a decision you're facing where two priorities conflict. How can you evaluate which option aligns best with your goals?

2. **Analyze a Past Decision:** Reflect on a trade-off you made previously. Was it successful? What could you improve?

3. **Set Guidelines:** Establish criteria to guide future trade-offs, ensuring they align with your core objectives.

Key Takeaway

Managing trade-offs with precision ensures that every decision aligns with your long-term goals. By carefully weighing priorities and acting deliberately, you maximize impact while minimizing regret.

Chapter 83: Engineer Irreversible Advantages

Irreversible advantages are the ultimate goal of strategic thinking. These advantages are not just temporary wins — they are enduring, defensible, and nearly impossible for competitors to replicate. When you engineer irreversible advantages, you position yourself, your team, or your organization in a way that ensures long-term dominance, even in the face of challenges or changing circumstances.

Creating such advantages requires a deep understanding of your unique strengths, market dynamics, and the specific needs of your audience. By combining these elements, you can establish a position that becomes your unshakable foundation for success.

Why Irreversible Advantages Matter

1. **Sustains Long-Term Success:** Once established, these advantages provide a consistent edge over competitors.

2. **Minimizes Threats:** Competitors are less likely to erode your position when your advantages are hard to replicate.

3. **Inspires Confidence:** Irreversible advantages attract loyal customers, partners, and stakeholders who value stability.

For example, companies that build strong intellectual property portfolios or establish exclusive partnerships create barriers that prevent others from easily entering their market space.

How to Engineer Irreversible Advantages

1. **Leverage Unique Strengths:** Identify what sets you apart and find ways to enhance and protect those qualities.

2. **Invest in Innovation:** Develop technologies, processes, or products that are difficult to copy.

3. **Strengthen Customer Loyalty:** Build trust and emotional connections with your audience to create long-term relationships.

4. **Establish Barriers to Entry:** Create systems, partnerships, or networks that make it challenging for competitors to enter your market.

5. **Focus on Scalability:** Design your advantages to grow with you, ensuring they remain effective as your goals evolve.

Real-World Example

John Deere, the agricultural equipment manufacturer, has engineered irreversible advantages by developing a comprehensive ecosystem of equipment, software, and data-driven services tailored to farmers' needs. Through innovations like precision agriculture technology and long-standing relationships with farming communities, John Deere has created barriers that competitors struggle to overcome. Farmers rely not just on their tractors but also on the integrated software and support systems, making John Deere an indispensable partner in their operations.

Exercises

1. **Identify Your Strengths:** List three qualities or resources that set you apart. How can you make them difficult to replicate?

2. **Spot Barriers to Entry:** Analyze your market. What unique systems or relationships can you develop to create barriers for competitors?

3. **Future-Proof Your Advantage:** Reflect on how your current strengths can scale with your goals. What adjustments are needed?

Key Takeaway

Engineering irreversible advantages ensures lasting success. By leveraging unique strengths, building barriers, and investing in innovation, you create a position that competitors cannot easily challenge.

Chapter 84: Use Authority to Multiply Impact

Authority, when used strategically, is a powerful multiplier of impact. It allows you to inspire trust, rally others behind your vision, and drive coordinated efforts toward a shared goal. Authority isn't about exercising control — it's about cultivating respect, credibility, and the ability to guide people effectively.

Leaders who use authority wisely amplify their influence and align resources efficiently. Whether it's inspiring a team, negotiating with stakeholders, or leading an organization, authority enables you to mobilize people and resources at scale, creating exponential results.

Why Authority Multiplies Impact

1. **Inspires Trust:** People follow leaders they respect, amplifying their ability to drive change.

2. **Unites Efforts:** Authority focuses diverse teams or stakeholders on shared objectives.

3. **Speeds Decision-Making:** Clear leadership eliminates confusion, allowing faster, more effective actions.

For example, CEOs with strong authority can implement organizational changes more effectively than leaders who struggle to gain buy-in from their teams.

How to Use Authority Strategically

1. **Build Credibility:** Establish yourself as a trustworthy and knowledgeable leader.
2. **Lead by Example:** Demonstrate the behaviors, values, and work ethic you want others to follow.
3. **Communicate Clearly:** Use your authority to provide clear direction and align efforts.
4. **Empower Others:** Delegate responsibilities and give your team the autonomy to succeed.
5. **Foster Relationships:** Cultivate mutual respect with stakeholders to strengthen your influence.

Real-World Example

In the late 2000s, Dave Lewis, former CEO of Tesco, used his authority to lead the UK-based supermarket chain through a critical turnaround. At the time, Tesco was struggling with declining market share, customer dissatisfaction, and internal inefficiencies.

Lewis immediately set out to restore trust with customers and employees by implementing a back-to-basics approach. He focused on improving customer service, enhancing product quality, and simplifying pricing strategies. His clear communication and decisive leadership helped rebuild Tesco's reputation and stabilize its operations, ultimately steering the company back to profitability.

Exercises

1. **Reflect on Your Authority:** Identify areas where your authority has the most impact. How can you use it more effectively?
2. **Strengthen Credibility:** List three actions you can take to build trust and respect among your peers or team.

3. **Empower Your Team:** Delegate a key responsibility to someone you trust. How can this amplify your collective impact?

Key Takeaway

Authority is a strategic tool for multiplying impact. By earning trust, aligning efforts, and empowering others, you create the conditions for exponential success.

Chapter 85: Turn Opponents' Strengths Into Vulnerabilities

One of the most overlooked strategies in competitive environments is turning your opponents' strengths into their vulnerabilities. Many organizations and individuals build their success around key advantages — whether it's their size, resources, reputation, or specialized expertise. However, these same strengths often come with limitations or blind spots that you can exploit to gain the upper hand.

This strategy requires more than recognizing your opponents' assets; it involves understanding the trade-offs that come with those assets. For example, large organizations may have vast resources but lack agility. Market leaders may dominate an industry but be slow to adopt innovation. By analyzing these dynamics, you can position yourself to use their strengths against them.

Why This Strategy Works

1. **Exploits Complacency:** Over-reliance on strengths can make opponents predictable or resistant to change.
2. **Highlights Weaknesses:** Strengths often come at the expense of flexibility, speed, or adaptability.
3. **Turns the Tables:** By using their own advantages against them, you can counterbalance power dynamics.

How to Turn Strengths Into Vulnerabilities

1. **Identify Overreliance:** Look for areas where opponents depend heavily on a single strength.
2. **Spot Inflexibility:** Assess whether their strengths make them slow to adapt to changing conditions.
3. **Position Yourself Strategically:** Use your own agility, creativity, or innovation to target their blind spots.
4. **Create Pressure Points:** Force them into situations where their strengths become liabilities, such as by emphasizing speed when they rely on scale.
5. **Be Unpredictable:** Avoid direct competition with their strength and instead operate where they are least prepared.

Real-World Example

When Aldi entered the U.S. market, it targeted grocery giants like Walmart. Instead of competing head-to-head on selection or store size, Aldi focused on its strength: simplicity. Its smaller stores and limited product lines allowed for lower costs, faster shopping experiences, and competitive pricing. Walmart's strength — offering massive selection — became a vulnerability as customers seeking convenience and affordability flocked to Aldi.

By exploiting the inefficiencies of their larger competitors, Aldi carved out a profitable niche and expanded rapidly in the U.S. market.

Exercises

1. **Analyze a Competitor's Strengths:** Identify one major strength of a competitor and consider how it could also limit their adaptability.

2. **Target a Blind Spot:** Think of a situation where you could use a competitor's strength to your advantage.

3. **Evaluate Your Own Strengths:** Reflect on your strengths and consider whether they leave you vulnerable to specific challenges.

Key Takeaway

Your opponents' strengths can often become their greatest vulnerabilities. By identifying blind spots and adapting your strategy accordingly, you can turn the tables and gain a significant advantage.

Chapter 86: Harness the Wisdom of the Crowd

The wisdom of the crowd is a powerful resource for solving complex problems, generating ideas, and making informed decisions. The collective knowledge, perspectives, and insights of a diverse group often produce better outcomes than those of any single individual, no matter how experienced or skilled. By harnessing this collective intelligence, you can unlock innovative solutions and gain deeper understanding in any situation.

Crowdsourcing ideas doesn't mean relying on random opinions. The key to leveraging the wisdom of the crowd lies in structuring the process effectively. When you curate input from diverse but informed perspectives, the aggregated knowledge becomes a strategic asset that far exceeds the sum of its parts.

Why the Wisdom of the Crowd Works

1. **Diversity Drives Insight:** A range of perspectives ensures you consider multiple angles and solutions.

2. **Aggregates Expertise:** Combining the knowledge of many people often leads to more accurate outcomes.

3. **Encourages Innovation:** Crowdsourced ideas can reveal creative solutions that one person might overlook.

For example, platforms like Wikipedia thrive on the collective contributions of users worldwide. By harnessing the expertise and dedication of a global crowd, Wikipedia has become one of the most comprehensive and trusted sources of knowledge.

How to Harness the Wisdom of the Crowd

1. **Define Your Goal:** Be clear about the problem you want to solve or the insight you want to gain.

2. **Gather a Diverse Group:** Include people with varied expertise, backgrounds, and perspectives.

3. **Encourage Open Participation:** Create an environment where everyone feels comfortable sharing their ideas.

4. **Aggregate and Analyze Data:** Look for patterns, trends, or commonalities in the input you receive.

5. **Test and Refine Solutions:** Use the crowd's insights as a starting point for developing actionable strategies.

Real-World Example

LEGO's Ideas platform is a brilliant example of using the wisdom of the crowd. LEGO invites fans to submit ideas for new sets, which are then reviewed by the company. Winning ideas, like the "LEGO Women of NASA" set, often become bestsellers. This approach not only generates innovative product ideas but also strengthens customer engagement by involving fans in the creative process.

Exercises

1. **Crowdsource an Idea:** Identify a challenge you're facing and gather input from a group of diverse individuals.

2. **Evaluate Collective Input:** Aggregate and analyze the suggestions you receive. What patterns emerge?

3. **Refine and Test:** Take one of the ideas from your crowdsource exercise and implement it on a small scale.

Key Takeaway

The wisdom of the crowd turns collective intelligence into a powerful strategic tool. By leveraging diverse perspectives, you gain deeper insights, foster innovation, and make better decisions.

Chapter 87: Command the Precision of Timing

Timing isn't just a factor in strategy — it's a force multiplier. Acting too early can lead to wasted resources, while acting too late often means missed opportunities. Commanding the precision of timing allows you to strike the perfect balance, ensuring that your actions create maximum impact.

Great strategists understand that timing is about more than speed; it's about aligning your actions with external factors like market readiness, competitor moves, or audience expectations. By mastering this balance, you can make decisions that not only meet the moment but also shape the future.

Why Timing is Crucial

1. **Maximizes Impact:** Acting at the right time amplifies your efforts and outcomes.
2. **Reduces Risk:** Careful timing ensures you avoid premature or poorly-timed actions.

3. **Creates Opportunities:** Observing the landscape helps you act when the conditions are most favorable.

For example, timing is critical in product launches. Introducing a product before a market is ready can result in failure, while waiting too long allows competitors to dominate. The key is finding the precise moment when demand aligns with readiness.

How to Command the Precision of Timing

1. **Monitor Trends:** Stay informed about industry shifts, market demands, and competitor activities.

2. **Evaluate Readiness:** Assess whether you, your team, and your resources are fully prepared to act.

3. **Wait for the Right Moment:** Be patient, but remain ready to act decisively when conditions align.

4. **Create Timing Windows:** Influence external factors, such as customer readiness or stakeholder interest, to align with your plans.

5. **Learn from History:** Study past successes and failures to understand how timing impacted outcomes.

Real-World Example

Zara, the global fashion retailer, is renowned for its precise timing in responding to fashion trends. Unlike competitors that plan collections months in advance, Zara's supply chain is designed to rapidly adapt to customer preferences. By monitoring sales data and consumer behavior in real time, Zara designs, manufactures, and delivers new items to stores in just a few weeks.

This ability to act at the right moment ensures Zara consistently aligns its offerings with current trends, keeping customers engaged and ahead of slower-moving competitors.

Exercises

1. **Reflect on Timing:** Think of a past decision. How did timing influence its success or failure?

2. **Identify a Key Moment:** Look at a current challenge or opportunity. When is the optimal time to act?

3. **Create a Timing Plan:** For an upcoming project, outline key milestones and external factors that will guide your timing decisions.

Key Takeaway

Precision in timing multiplies the effectiveness of your actions. By carefully monitoring trends, evaluating readiness, and acting decisively, you align your strategy with the perfect moment for success.

Chapter 88: Uncover Unique Perspectives to Lead with an Edge

Standing out requires more than just good ideas — it requires unique perspectives. Leaders who uncover fresh ways of thinking gain a powerful edge, allowing them to see opportunities others miss, solve problems innovatively, and inspire teams to achieve extraordinary results.

Uncovering unique perspectives involves seeking out diverse inputs, challenging assumptions, and being open to unconventional approaches. It's not just about being different for the sake of it; it's about finding new angles that unlock value and create meaningful impact.

Why Unique Perspectives Matter

1. **Drives Innovation:** Fresh viewpoints reveal creative solutions to entrenched challenges.

2. **Builds Competitive Advantage:** Seeing what others overlook positions you ahead of the curve.

3. **Fosters Growth:** Diverse thinking encourages adaptability and learning.

For example, many breakthroughs in business come from leaders who apply ideas from one industry to another. Cross-pollinating perspectives often leads to innovations that redefine markets.

How to Uncover Unique Perspectives

1. **Seek Diverse Inputs:** Collaborate with people from different backgrounds, industries, or cultures.

2. **Challenge Conventional Thinking:** Question assumptions and explore alternative viewpoints.

3. **Experiment Freely:** Test unconventional ideas on a small scale to gauge their potential.

4. **Look Outside Your Industry:** Study trends and practices in unrelated fields for transferable insights.

5. **Encourage Open Dialogue:** Foster a team culture where unconventional ideas are welcomed and explored.

Real-World Example

Chipotle revolutionized the fast-food industry by combining high-quality, fresh ingredients with the efficiency of a quick-service restaurant. Inspired by fine dining concepts and the growing demand for healthier options, Chipotle's unique perspective broke away from traditional fast-food norms. This differentiation helped the brand carve out a new niche in the industry, known as "fast-casual dining."

Exercises

1. **Challenge Assumptions:** Identify a current problem and list three assumptions you've made about it. How could they be wrong?

2. **Collaborate Outside Your Comfort Zone:** Partner with someone from a different field or background for fresh insights.

3. **Explore Other Industries:** Research trends in an industry unrelated to yours. What lessons can you apply?

Key Takeaway

Unique perspectives give you a competitive edge by revealing opportunities and solutions others overlook. By fostering diverse thinking and challenging assumptions, you position yourself to lead innovatively and effectively.

Chapter 89: Be Relentless in Follow-Through

A brilliant strategy means little without relentless follow-through. It's not the initial idea or effort that determines success — it's the consistent, determined execution that brings results. Being relentless in follow-through means committing to your goals, overcoming obstacles, and staying focused even when challenges arise.

Follow-through isn't just about persistence; it's about strategic persistence. It involves revisiting your plan, adjusting your approach when needed, and continuously pushing toward the finish line. This disciplined focus sets leaders and organizations apart in competitive landscapes where distractions and setbacks are inevitable.

Why Follow-Through is Essential

1. **Transforms Ideas into Results:** Execution turns vision into tangible outcomes.

2. **Builds Credibility:** Consistently delivering on promises earns trust and respect.

3. **Fosters Resilience:** Persistent follow-through helps you adapt and overcome challenges.

For example, many start-ups fail not because of flawed ideas but because they lack the discipline to follow through consistently. Relentless execution bridges the gap between potential and achievement.

How to Be Relentless in Follow-Through

1. **Set Clear Milestones:** Break down your goals into manageable steps and track your progress.

2. **Stay Focused:** Avoid distractions and stay committed to your objectives.

3. **Adapt to Challenges:** Be flexible in your approach but firm in your commitment to the goal.

4. **Hold Yourself Accountable:** Regularly evaluate your actions and adjust where needed.

5. **Celebrate Progress:** Recognize small victories to maintain motivation and momentum.

Real-World Example

Nike's global dominance is a testament to relentless follow-through. From the launch of its first running shoes in the 1960s to its transformation into a lifestyle brand, Nike has consistently executed on its vision of inspiring athletes. Campaigns such as "Just Do It" reinforced its brand identity, while ongoing innovation in footwear and apparel ensured market leadership. Nike's commitment to execution — through design, marketing, and partnerships — has made it a leader for decades.

Exercises

1. **Evaluate Your Persistence:** Reflect on a recent project. Did you follow through to completion? If not, identify what stopped you.

2. **Set Milestones:** Break down a current goal into smaller steps and create a timeline to track progress.

3. **Commit Publicly:** Share your goal with a trusted friend or colleague to create accountability for follow-through.

Key Takeaway

Relentless follow-through transforms vision into reality. By staying focused, adaptable, and committed, you ensure that your efforts deliver meaningful and lasting results.

Chapter 90: Apply the Prisoner's Dilemma to Real Life

The Prisoner's Dilemma, a classic concept from game theory, illustrates how individuals must balance self-interest with collaboration in situations where trust is uncertain. In this scenario, two individuals must choose to cooperate or betray each other, with outcomes dependent on their decisions. While mutual cooperation yields the best results for both, fear of betrayal often leads to suboptimal choices.

In real life, this dilemma plays out in negotiations, partnerships, and competitive environments. Understanding and applying the Prisoner's Dilemma allows you to anticipate behaviors, foster trust, and make decisions that maximize long-term gains.

Why Understanding the Prisoner's Dilemma is Valuable

1. **Improves Decision-Making:** Recognizing the dynamics of cooperation and competition helps you act strategically.
2. **Builds Trust:** Choosing cooperation in the right scenarios fosters stronger relationships.
3. **Prevents Exploitation:** Knowing when to protect your interests guards against betrayal.

For example, businesses in the same industry often face this dilemma. Should they compete aggressively or collaborate to expand the market? Balancing these choices strategically determines long-term outcomes.

How to Apply the Prisoner's Dilemma

1. **Assess Incentives:** Identify the rewards and risks for cooperation versus competition.
2. **Foster Communication:** Open dialogue reduces uncertainty and builds trust.
3. **Promote Mutual Benefits:** Highlight the advantages of working together to encourage cooperation.
4. **Use Tit-for-Tat Strategies:** In repeat interactions, start by cooperating and respond to the other party's actions accordingly.
5. **Analyze Long-Term Outcomes:** Focus on decisions that benefit you over multiple interactions rather than a single event.

Real-World Example

In the 1990s, Intel and AMD faced a classic Prisoner's Dilemma in the semiconductor industry. While they competed fiercely, both companies realized that setting certain standards, such as x86 processor compatibility, benefited the entire industry by fostering broader adoption of personal computers. This strategic cooperation allowed both companies to grow, even as they remained competitors.

Exercises

1. **Identify a Dilemma:** Think of a situation where you face a choice between collaboration and self-interest. What factors will influence your decision?

2. **Simulate the Scenario:** Role-play a Prisoner's Dilemma with a colleague to explore strategies for cooperation and competition.

3. **Reflect on Long-Term Gains:** Analyze a past decision. Did focusing on short-term benefits lead to better or worse outcomes?

Key Takeaway

Applying the Prisoner's Dilemma to real life helps you navigate trust and competition effectively. By fostering collaboration in the right contexts and protecting your interests strategically, you create outcomes that benefit all parties involved.

Chapter 91: Engineer Scarcity to Drive Value

Scarcity is one of the most powerful drivers of value. When something is rare, hard to obtain, or available only for a limited time, its desirability skyrockets. People are wired to value what they perceive as exclusive or fleeting, and strategic use of scarcity can elevate your offerings, strengthen demand, and position your brand as premium.

Engineering scarcity isn't about creating artificial shortages—it's about carefully controlling supply, timing, or accessibility to enhance perceived value. When done effectively, scarcity not only increases demand but also fosters a sense of urgency, prompting quicker decision-making from your audience.

Why Scarcity Works

1. **Increases Perceived Value:** People often equate rarity with quality or significance.

2. **Drives Urgency:** Limited availability prompts quicker action to avoid missing out.

3. **Encourages Exclusivity:** Scarcity creates a sense of being part of an elite group, enhancing loyalty and engagement.

For example, many luxury brands like Hermès limit the availability of their products, such as the iconic Birkin bag. This scarcity not only drives demand but also strengthens the brand's image as exclusive and aspirational.

How to Engineer Scarcity

1. **Limit Supply:** Offer a controlled quantity of products or services to create exclusivity.

2. **Create Time Constraints:** Use limited-time offers or seasonal releases to drive urgency.

3. **Segment Access:** Provide early or exclusive access to loyal customers or members.

4. **Highlight Rarity:** Clearly communicate why the opportunity is unique or hard to find.

5. **Avoid Artificiality:** Ensure your scarcity strategy feels authentic, not manipulative.

Real-World Example

The book publishing industry often uses scarcity to great effect. J.K. Rowling's *The Tales of Beedle the Bard* was initially released as a limited edition, with only seven handwritten copies. This exclusivity generated immense interest, making the eventual mass-market release a major event. The combination of scarcity and anticipation heightened the book's value and appeal.

Exercises

1. **Identify an Opportunity for Scarcity:** Choose a product or service you offer. How can you limit its availability or timing to enhance its value?

2. **Analyze Competitor Strategies:** Look at how competitors use scarcity. What lessons can you apply to your approach?

3. **Test a Scarcity Strategy:** Run a limited-time or exclusive offering and track its impact on engagement and sales.

Key Takeaway

Scarcity is a strategic tool that elevates value and drives demand. By carefully limiting supply, timing, or access, you create urgency and exclusivity that resonates with your audience.

Chapter 92: Use Game-Theoretic Modeling to Predict Next Steps

Game theory is the science of strategic interaction. It provides a framework for predicting how individuals or groups will behave in competitive or cooperative situations. By applying game-theoretic modeling, you can anticipate the actions of others, optimize your decisions, and gain an edge in complex environments.

Game theory isn't just for mathematicians—it's a practical tool for decision-making in business, politics, negotiations, and more. It helps you map out scenarios, assess risks, and identify optimal strategies by considering the motivations and potential responses of all parties involved.

Why Game Theory is Powerful

1. **Enhances Prediction:** Understanding others' incentives helps you anticipate their moves.
2. **Improves Decision-Making:** Game theory provides a structured approach to analyzing complex scenarios.

3. **Reveals Hidden Opportunities:** By modeling interactions, you often uncover win-win solutions or strategic advantages.

For example, game theory is frequently applied in auction design. Governments and companies use it to structure bidding processes that maximize value while ensuring fair competition.

How to Use Game-Theoretic Modeling

1. **Define the Players:** Identify all parties involved in the situation.
2. **Clarify Incentives:** Understand the goals and motivations of each player.
3. **Map Possible Moves:** List the potential actions each player could take.
4. **Analyze Outcomes:** Evaluate the consequences of each combination of moves.
5. **Select Your Strategy:** Choose the option that best aligns with your goals while anticipating others' responses.

Real-World Example

Procter & Gamble (P&G) used game theory to address competition in the detergent market. Facing aggressive pricing strategies from rivals, P&G analyzed how competitors would react to various pricing and product decisions. Using game-theoretic modeling, they anticipated that rivals would respond aggressively to price cuts but less so to product innovation.

P&G shifted its focus to launching Tide Pods, an innovative product that created a new market segment. This move allowed P&G to gain a competitive edge without engaging in damaging price wars, demonstrating the power of game theory in predicting and influencing market dynamics.

Exercises

1. **Identify a Strategic Interaction:** Think of a competitive or cooperative situation you're facing. Who are the players, and what are their incentives?

2. **Model Possible Moves:** Map out the potential actions of each party and the likely outcomes.
3. **Test a Strategy:** Choose a course of action based on your analysis and monitor the results.

Key Takeaway

Game-theoretic modeling provides a strategic edge by predicting others' actions and optimizing your decisions. By understanding incentives and mapping scenarios, you stay one step ahead in complex interactions.

Chapter 93: Identify and Gain from Bottlenecks in Systems

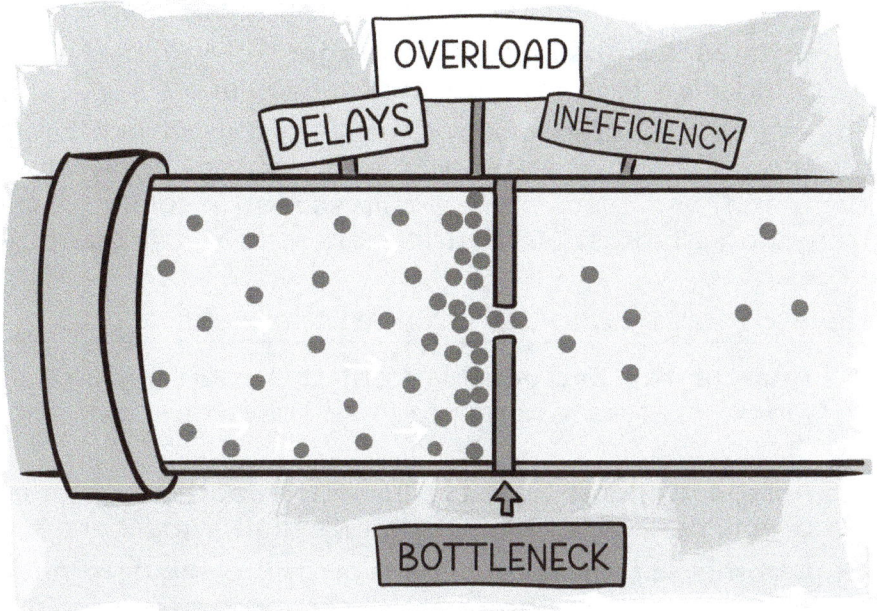

Bottlenecks are the points in a system where progress slows, efficiency drops, or resources are constrained. While they're often seen as obstacles, bottlenecks can also present opportunities. Identifying and addressing these constraints allows you to unlock hidden potential, improve system performance, and even gain a competitive edge by solving problems others overlook.

Whether in supply chains, workflows, or decision-making processes, bottlenecks are inevitable. The key is to approach them strategically. Instead of working around or ignoring them, focus on understanding their root causes and finding ways to improve or bypass them. By doing so, you turn limitations into opportunities for growth and innovation.

Why Addressing Bottlenecks Matters

1. **Maximizes Efficiency:** Removing constraints allows systems to flow more smoothly and productively.
2. **Improves Decision-Making:** Identifying critical points clarifies where resources and attention are needed most.
3. **Creates Competitive Advantage:** Solving bottlenecks often leads to innovations that set you apart.

For example, bottlenecks in logistics systems, such as port congestion, can delay shipments and disrupt supply chains. Addressing these issues often requires creative solutions, such as rerouting shipments or using alternative transportation methods.

How to Identify and Gain from Bottlenecks

1. **Analyze the System:** Map out the entire process and pinpoint areas where progress slows or inefficiencies occur.
2. **Assess Impact:** Evaluate how the bottleneck affects overall performance and prioritize high-impact areas.
3. **Optimize or Eliminate:** Focus on improving or removing the bottleneck through better processes, tools, or resources.
4. **Innovate Around Constraints:** Use the bottleneck as inspiration to develop alternative methods or solutions.
5. **Monitor Continuously:** Bottlenecks can shift over time, so regular analysis is essential.

Real-World Example

In the early 2000s, Dell Computers faced bottlenecks in its supply chain that were slowing production and increasing costs. To address this, Dell restructured its operations by adopting a build-to-order model. Instead of relying on large inventories, Dell began producing computers only after receiving customer orders.

This approach eliminated delays caused by excess inventory and reduced dependency on forecast accuracy. By streamlining its supply chain and focusing on real-time demand, Dell not only removed a significant bottleneck but also gained a competitive edge by delivering customized products faster than competitors.

Exercises

1. **Map a Process:** Choose a workflow or system you're involved with. Identify the step where progress slows most frequently.

2. **Evaluate Solutions:** Brainstorm three ways to address a bottleneck in your current system. Which option offers the best balance of effort and impact?

3. **Measure Impact:** Implement one solution and track the improvement in efficiency or performance.

Key Takeaway

Bottlenecks are opportunities in disguise. By identifying constraints and optimizing around them, you unlock hidden potential and position yourself for sustained success.

Chapter 94: Redefine the Rules of the Game

In a competitive environment, playing by the established rules often leads to incremental progress at best. To truly stand out, you must redefine the rules of the game. This strategy involves changing the parameters of competition to favor your strengths, creating a playing field where you have the upper hand.

Redefining the rules doesn't mean breaking them —it means reshaping expectations, challenging assumptions, and introducing innovations that others must adapt to. When you set the standard, competitors must follow your lead, allowing you to dictate the pace and direction of the industry.

Why Redefining the Rules Works

1. **Creates a New Playing Field:** Changing the rules forces competitors to adapt to your terms.
2. **Highlights Strengths:** By redefining the game, you emphasize your unique advantages.

3. **Inspires Innovation:** Breaking free from tradition fosters creative solutions and opportunities.

For example, when Cirque du Soleil entered the entertainment market, it redefined the circus. By eliminating animals, focusing on theatrical storytelling, and targeting adult audiences, Cirque created a new category of performance art. This shift allowed it to thrive in a declining industry while leaving traditional circuses scrambling to catch up.

How to Redefine the Rules

1. **Question Assumptions:** Challenge the norms and traditions that define your industry or field.
2. **Identify Your Strengths:** Focus on what sets you apart and build your strategy around those advantages.
3. **Introduce Innovations:** Develop products, services, or approaches that disrupt expectations.
4. **Change the Narrative:** Use branding and communication to frame your approach as the new standard.
5. **Lead the Transition:** Help stakeholders and customers embrace the new rules through education and engagement.

Real-World Example

Warby Parker redefined the eyewear industry by introducing an innovative direct-to-consumer model. Traditional glasses retailers relied on high markups, in-store fittings, and limited selection. Warby Parker flipped the script by offering stylish, affordable frames online with a home try-on program. This approach disrupted the industry and forced competitors to adapt to the new customer expectations Warby Parker had established.

Exercises

1. **Challenge a Norm:** Identify one "rule" in your industry or field. How could you approach it differently?
2. **Highlight Your Edge:** List three unique strengths you have. How can you use them to redefine expectations?

3. **Test a New Rule:** Implement a small change in how you operate and assess its impact on your environment.

Key Takeaway

Redefining the rules of the game transforms competition into opportunity. By reshaping expectations and introducing innovations, you position yourself to lead and thrive on your terms.

Chapter 95: Turn Opposing Forces Into Complementors

In competitive environments, it's easy to view opposing forces solely as adversaries. However, there are situations where your competitors or seemingly conflicting elements can become valuable partners. Turning opposing forces into complementors involves finding ways to align interests, leveraging each other's strengths, and creating win-win scenarios that benefit everyone involved.

This strategy requires a shift in mindset — rather than focusing on defeating your opponent, you unlock opportunities for mutual growth, shared innovation, and enhanced market reach.

Why This Strategy Works

1. **Unlocks Synergy:** Combining strengths with others often leads to greater collective impact.

2. **Expands Opportunities:** Collaboration opens doors to resources, networks, or markets you couldn't access alone.

3. **Reduces Conflict:** Aligning interests minimizes competition and creates a more cooperative dynamic.

For example, rival tech companies often collaborate on setting industry standards, benefiting both parties while fostering innovation that drives the entire sector forward.

How to Turn Opposing Forces Into Complementors

1. **Identify Shared Goals:** Look for areas where your interests align with your competitors or opposing forces.

2. **Focus on Strengths:** Leverage what each party brings to the table to create a stronger partnership.

3. **Define Boundaries:** Set clear terms to ensure collaboration remains mutually beneficial.

4. **Communicate Openly:** Foster trust and transparency to build a sustainable relationship.

5. **Monitor and Adjust:** Continuously evaluate the partnership to ensure it stays aligned with your objectives.

Real-World Example

Rival automakers BMW and Mercedes-Benz collaborated in 2015 to create Here, a digital mapping platform for autonomous driving. While traditionally fierce competitors, they recognized that pooling resources to develop advanced mapping technology would benefit both companies. By collaborating on this shared goal, they accelerated innovation and positioned themselves as leaders in the evolving field of autonomous vehicles.

Exercises

1. **Identify a Potential Complementor:** Think of a competitor or opposing force in your industry. What shared goals could you explore?

2. **Map Collaborative Opportunities:** List three areas where combining resources or expertise with an opposing force could create mutual benefit.

3. **Test the Waters:** Propose a small-scale collaboration to gauge feasibility and trust.

Key Takeaway

Turning opposing forces into complementors transforms competition into opportunity. By aligning shared goals and leveraging mutual strengths, you create partnerships that benefit all involved and expand the potential for success.

Chapter 96: Always Leave Room for Reversal

Even the best-laid plans can face unforeseen challenges, and rigidity in strategy often leads to failure. Always leaving room for reversal ensures that you have the flexibility to pivot, adapt, or even undo decisions when circumstances change. This principle is not about abandoning commitment — it's about building adaptability into your approach to safeguard against uncertainty.

Reversals can be difficult, but they often prevent greater losses or open up new opportunities. A willingness to change direction signals strength and strategic foresight, not weakness. By preparing for potential reversals, you ensure that you're never locked into a path that no longer serves your goals.

Why Reversal is Essential

1. **Reduces Risk:** Flexibility minimizes the impact of unforeseen challenges.

2. **Encourages Innovation:** The ability to pivot fosters creativity and experimentation.
3. **Preserves Resources:** Reversals often prevent further losses when a strategy proves ineffective.

For example, businesses launching new products often build in the option to discontinue or rebrand if early results don't meet expectations. This approach allows them to experiment without committing irreversibly to a failing course.

How to Leave Room for Reversal

1. **Start Small:** Test ideas on a limited scale before committing significant resources.
2. **Set Decision Gates:** Define checkpoints where you evaluate progress and decide whether to continue, pivot, or reverse.
3. **Build Flexibility:** Design strategies and processes that allow for adjustments without significant disruption.
4. **Monitor Continuously:** Stay attuned to changes in your environment, competitors, and results.
5. **Communicate Openly:** Ensure that stakeholders understand the importance of adaptability and are prepared for potential reversals.

Real-World Example

The food company Campbell's launched its low-sodium soups in response to growing health trends. However, when sales declined due to customer dissatisfaction with taste, Campbell's reversed its strategy by reintroducing the original recipes while maintaining a smaller low-sodium product line. This flexibility preserved its brand reputation and allowed the company to meet diverse customer needs.

Exercises

1. **Analyze a Current Plan:** Identify a strategy where you could incorporate more flexibility for reversal.
2. **Evaluate Past Decisions:** Reflect on a situation where leaving room for reversal could have improved the outcome.

3. **Design a Safety Net:** Develop a contingency plan for a current project or decision.

Key Takeaway

Leaving room for reversal ensures that you remain adaptable in the face of change. By building flexibility into your strategies, you protect your goals and stay prepared for unexpected challenges.

Chapter 97: Stockpile Reserves for Important Moments

In strategy, timing is everything — but timing without resources is wasted potential. Stockpiling reserves ensures that when the right moment arises, you have the means to act decisively and effectively. These reserves could be financial capital, talent, energy, or even goodwill, ready to deploy when the stakes are highest.

Reserves aren't just about survival; they're about seizing opportunities. When competitors are overextended or markets are volatile, your ability to act from a position of strength becomes a game-changer. By strategically building and managing reserves, you prepare not just for challenges but also for the moments that define long-term success.

Why Stockpiling Reserves is Critical

1. **Provides Stability:** Reserves act as a buffer against unexpected setbacks.

2. **Enables Strategic Action:** Having resources ready allows you to act quickly when opportunities arise.

3. **Builds Resilience:** Preparedness fosters confidence and adaptability in uncertain environments.

For example, companies that maintain financial reserves can invest in innovation or acquisitions during economic downturns, while competitors struggle to stay afloat.

How to Stockpile Reserves Strategically

1. **Identify Key Resources:** Determine what types of reserves are most valuable for your goals (e.g., funds, relationships, materials).

2. **Build Gradually:** Accumulate reserves consistently, even during stable periods, to avoid overextension.

3. **Protect Against Overuse:** Establish clear criteria for when and how reserves can be deployed.

4. **Align with Goals:** Ensure your reserves directly support your long-term objectives.

5. **Monitor Regularly:** Track your reserves to ensure they remain sufficient and relevant.

Real-World Example

Costco has long been recognized for its disciplined approach to inventory management. Unlike many retailers that run lean to minimize costs, Costco stockpiles essential goods in larger quantities. This strategy allowed Costco to maintain availability and meet customer demand during supply chain disruptions, reinforcing customer loyalty and market stability.

Exercises

1. **Assess Your Reserves:** Identify the resources you currently have and where gaps exist.

2. **Develop a Stockpiling Plan:** Create a strategy for gradually building reserves without overextending.

3. **Set Usage Criteria:** Define the conditions under which reserves can be used to maximize impact.

Key Takeaway

Stockpiling reserves prepares you for both challenges and opportunities. By building and managing key resources strategically, you ensure the ability to act decisively when it matters most.

Chapter 98: Design Self-Reinforcing Systems

Self-reinforcing systems are the ultimate strategic advantage. These systems create a positive feedback loop where each success strengthens the next, driving continuous improvement and growth. When designed effectively, they reduce effort over time while producing increasingly significant results.

This strategy requires careful planning. Self-reinforcing systems thrive on alignment—where inputs and outputs are connected in a way that creates momentum. By identifying key areas where your efforts can compound, you set the foundation for sustainable progress that builds on itself.

Why Self-Reinforcing Systems Work

1. **Creates Momentum:** Positive feedback loops accelerate progress with minimal additional effort.
2. **Drives Efficiency:** Automation and scalability reduce resource expenditure over time.

3. **Builds Resilience:** Strong systems withstand external shocks and adapt to change.

For example, loyalty programs like those offered by Sephora encourage repeat purchases by rewarding customers. The more customers buy, the more rewards they earn, which incentivizes further engagement — fueling the company's growth while deepening customer loyalty.

How to Design Self-Reinforcing Systems

1. **Identify Core Drivers:** Pinpoint the actions or inputs that create the most significant results.

2. **Connect Inputs and Outputs:** Ensure that each success feeds back into the system, creating a loop of reinforcement.

3. **Leverage Technology:** Automate processes to enhance scalability and reduce manual intervention.

4. **Evaluate Scalability:** Test the system's ability to grow without losing effectiveness.

5. **Monitor and Adjust:** Continuously assess the system's performance and make improvements as needed.

Real-World Example

The video game company Epic Games, creators of *Fortnite*, has built a self-reinforcing system through its free-to-play model and in-game purchases. By offering *Fortnite* for free, the company attracted millions of players. These players, in turn, purchase cosmetic upgrades and skins, generating substantial revenue without impacting gameplay balance.

Epic reinvests this revenue into frequent content updates, events, and collaborations, which keep players engaged and attract new ones. The growing player base further enhances the game's community and visibility, creating a feedback loop that continually strengthens *Fortnite's* position as a global gaming phenomenon.

Exercises

1. **Identify a Potential Loop:** Reflect on one area of your work or business where a feedback loop could create compounding results.

2. **Map the System:** Outline how inputs and outputs can connect to reinforce each other.
3. **Test and Refine:** Implement a small-scale version of your system and assess its impact.

Key Takeaway

Self-reinforcing systems create sustainable, scalable success. By designing processes that compound results, you build momentum and efficiency that drive long-term growth.

Chapter 99: End Games with Grace and Foresight

In strategy, how you end matters as much as how you begin. Whether it's concluding a negotiation, exiting a market, or wrapping up a long-term project, the final steps often define perceptions, relationships, and future opportunities. Ending with grace and foresight ensures that you leave on your terms, maintain credibility, and set the stage for what comes next.

End games require careful planning. While it's tempting to focus solely on achieving your goal, a poorly executed exit can undo years of progress. Thoughtful conclusions consider both immediate results and long-term implications, balancing the need for closure with the potential for future growth.

Why Ending Gracefully Matters

1. **Preserves Relationships:** Leaving with respect and professionalism strengthens connections for future collaborations.

2. **Enhances Reputation:** A well-executed conclusion reinforces your credibility and legacy.

3. **Opens New Doors:** Strategic endings often lead to fresh opportunities or smoother transitions.

For example, businesses that phase out obsolete products responsibly—offering clear communication and support to customers—maintain loyalty and pave the way for their next innovation.

How to End with Grace and Foresight

1. **Define Success Early:** Establish clear goals for your conclusion, ensuring alignment with your long-term vision.

2. **Communicate Transparently:** Keep stakeholders informed about your decisions and next steps.

3. **Minimize Disruption:** Take steps to ensure smooth transitions and avoid unnecessary complications.

4. **Reflect and Document:** Analyze what worked, what didn't, and how lessons learned can inform future efforts.

5. **Leave the Door Open:** Conclude with positivity, leaving room for future opportunities or collaborations.

Real-World Example

General Electric (GE) decided to exit its lighting business after over a century of operation. Instead of abruptly shutting down, GE transitioned its lighting division to a buyer while ensuring employees and customers were supported throughout the process. This graceful exit preserved GE's reputation while allowing it to focus on more profitable sectors.

Exercises

1. **Plan an Exit:** Identify one project or commitment nearing completion. How can you conclude it thoughtfully and strategically?

2. **Reflect on Past Endings:** Think of a situation where you ended something poorly. What could you have done differently?

3. **Set Closing Goals:** For an ongoing effort, define what success looks like at the end and how you'll achieve it.

Key Takeaway

Ending with grace and foresight ensures that your conclusions are as strategic as your beginnings. By focusing on professionalism, reflection, and future potential, you close the chapter while setting the stage for continued success.

Chapter 100: Achieve Strategic Mastery Through Continuous Education

Mastery is not a destination but a journey. The most successful strategists understand that learning never ends. Whether you're refining your skills, exploring new concepts, or adapting to an evolving world, continuous education is the key to staying relevant, innovative, and ahead of the curve.

Strategic mastery isn't just about accumulating knowledge — it's about applying it. Each new insight builds on what you already know, deepening your understanding and expanding your capabilities. By committing to lifelong learning, you ensure that your strategies remain fresh, adaptable, and effective in any environment.

Why Continuous Education is Essential

1. **Keeps You Relevant:** Staying informed ensures you're always prepared for emerging trends and challenges.

2. **Enhances Innovation:** New ideas and perspectives fuel creativity and growth.
3. **Builds Confidence:** Ongoing learning reinforces your expertise, making you a more decisive and effective leader.

For example, many leaders dedicate time to reading, attending workshops, or engaging in peer networks to stay updated on best practices and industry shifts.

How to Pursue Continuous Education

1. **Stay Curious:** Regularly seek out new topics, books, or courses that challenge your current understanding.
2. **Learn from Experience:** Reflect on successes and failures to extract valuable lessons.
3. **Engage with Experts:** Build relationships with mentors or peers who can offer diverse perspectives.
4. **Experiment and Apply:** Test new strategies or ideas in low-risk scenarios to refine your skills.
5. **Commit to Growth:** Set specific goals for your personal and professional development.

Real-World Example

The late Ruth Bader Ginsburg, U.S. Supreme Court Justice, exemplified continuous education. Even as a highly accomplished legal mind, she consistently sought new knowledge, from studying emerging legal theories to engaging with cultural and technological shifts. Her commitment to lifelong learning allowed her to remain a relevant and transformative figure in her field.

Exercises

1. **Identify Learning Goals:** Write down three areas where you want to expand your knowledge or skills.
2. **Schedule Learning Time:** Dedicate a specific time each week to reading, attending events, or exploring new ideas.
3. **Test Your Knowledge:** Apply a new concept or skill in your work to see how it enhances your strategy.

Key Takeaway

Strategic mastery is built through continuous education. By staying curious, reflective, and open to new ideas, you ensure that your strategies remain dynamic, effective, and ahead of the curve.

Conclusion

This book has explored 100 strategies to empower you with the tools needed to think, act, and lead strategically in an ever-changing world. Each chapter was designed to guide you from foundational principles to advanced concepts, providing insights that apply across industries, challenges, and ambitions. Now, the challenge is to integrate them into your decision-making processes, leadership style, and long-term vision.

From Knowledge to Action

Strategic thinking isn't just about knowing what to do; it's about consistently applying these principles to achieve your goals. Start small. Implement one or two strategies that feel most actionable, measure their impact, and refine your approach. Strategy is iterative — it evolves as you learn and adapt. By starting with focused actions and expanding gradually, you build confidence and momentum that carry you forward.

Adapting to Complexity

A critical aspect of strategic mastery is knowing when to pivot. As circumstances change, strategies that once worked may need to be re-evaluated. Leaving room for reversal, testing assumptions, and applying feedback loops ensure that you remain flexible and ready to adjust when needed. Remember, agility and foresight are your greatest allies in a world of constant change.

Applying the Lessons in Every Sphere

The strategies in this book aren't limited to business or professional endeavors — they apply to every aspect of life. Whether you're negotiating with a partner, planning a personal project, or navigating complex relationships, these lessons provide tools for better decision-making, clearer communication, and more effective action.

For example, concepts such as prioritizing clarity over speed, aligning incentives, and fostering mutual dependence can improve teamwork and relationships. Similarly, strategies like leveraging asymmetry and anticipating trends help you stay ahead in personal or professional growth.

Looking Ahead

Now it's your turn. Take these strategies and make them your own. Use them to shape your decisions, inspire your team, and achieve your goals. Reflect on what you've learned, stay open to growth, and lead with purpose and precision.

Appendix A: Quick Reference Guide

This appendix is your go-to resource for a concise overview of the strategies covered in the book. Each chapter has been summarized into a single actionable line, allowing you to revisit key insights at a glance. Use this section as a quick reference to remind yourself of the tools and concepts you've learned, organized by the five parts of the book.

Part 1: Foundational Strategies

1. **Play the Long Game, Not the Next Move:** Focus on sustainable, long-term success over short-term wins.

2. **Begin with the End in Mind:** Start every strategy with a clear vision of your ultimate goal.

3. **Prioritize Clarity Over Speed:** Make decisions with precision rather than rushing into action.

4. **Leverage Asymmetry in Resources:** Use unique advantages to outperform competitors with greater resources.

5. **Embrace Iterative Progress:** Build success gradually through small, consistent improvements.

6. **Balance Offensive and Defensive Moves:** Blend proactive and protective strategies for well-rounded success.

7. **Understand the Zero-Sum Game:** Recognize when competition requires gaining at others' expense.

8. **Find Win-Win Opportunities:** Seek collaborative solutions that benefit all parties involved.

9. **Evaluate Trade-Offs in Every Decision:** Weigh costs and benefits to optimize outcomes.

10. **Don't Confuse Luck with Strategy:** Separate chance from deliberate planning to refine your approach.

11. **Cultivate Tactical Patience:** Wait for the right opportunity before taking action.

12. **Harness the Power of Perception:** Use how others see you to influence outcomes in your favor.

13. **Simplify Complex Options:** Break down overwhelming choices into clear, actionable steps.

14. **Always Ask "Why?" Twice:** Dig deeper into motivations and assumptions to uncover the truth.

15. **Avoid Overcommitting Help:** Offer assistance wisely to prevent resource overextension.

16. **Be the First Mover When It Counts:** Act early to seize opportunities or shape the playing field.

17. **Follow the Nash Equilibrium:** Make decisions that balance individual and collective gains.

18. **Build Redundancies for Resilience:** Prepare for uncertainty by creating backup systems.

19. **Don't Neglect the Cost of Inaction:** Recognize the risks of staying idle in a changing landscape.

20. **Master the Pivot Point:** Adapt quickly and effectively when plans need to change.

Part 2: Competitive Strategies

21. **Make the Most of Your Competition's Blind Spots:** Exploit gaps in your competitors' awareness to gain an edge.

22. **Focus on the Player, Not Just the Rules:** Tailor your strategy to your opponent's behavior, not just the framework.

23. **Control the Tempo of Engagement:** Set the pace of interactions to stay in control.

24. **Feign Weakness Where You Are Strong:** Mislead competitors by disguising your strengths.

25. **Cultivate Alliances to Outflank Threats:** Partner with others to neutralize shared challenges.

26. **Use Decoys to Distract and Mislead:** Divert attention from your true intentions to gain an advantage.

27. **Capture High Ground in Negotiations:** Secure leverage by framing discussions in your favor.

28. **Create False Choices to Frame the Narrative:** Shape decisions by limiting perceived options.

29. **Use a Divide-and-Conquer Approach:** Fragment opponents to weaken their collective strength.

30. **Benefit from the Overconfidence of Your Opponents:** Capitalize on rivals' overestimations of their abilities.

31. **Pre-empt Competitors Through Purposeful Partnerships:** Collaborate to block competitors before they act.

32. **Set Traps by Shaping Expectations:** Lead opponents into predictable, disadvantageous actions.

33. **Win Battles, Avoid Wars:** Prioritize focused victories over costly, drawn-out conflicts.

34. **Undermine Rivals with Incremental Disruption:** Erode competitors' strengths through small, consistent moves.

35. **Neutralize Emerging Risks Before They Escalate:** Address potential threats early to prevent larger issues.

36. **Channel Psychological Momentum:** Use confidence and timing to keep the advantage on your side.

37. **Adopt an Inside-Out Mindset:** Leverage internal strengths before looking outward for solutions.

38. **Counter Aggression with Calm Confidence:** Respond to threats with poise to neutralize their impact.

39. **Force Your Competitors to Overextend:** Encourage rivals to exhaust resources while you stay steady.

40. **Apply the Minimax Principle in Critical Decisions:** Minimize potential losses while maximizing gains.

Part 3: Cooperative Strategies

41. **Lay the Foundation for Trust Before You Request Collaboration:** Build credibility before seeking cooperation.

42. **Bolster Mutual Dependence in Joint Ventures:** Strengthen interdependence to ensure partnership success.

43. **Share the Pie to Make It Bigger:** Expand opportunities by collaborating rather than competing.

44. **Use Reciprocity to Strengthen Relationships:** Foster goodwill by giving value before seeking returns.

45. **Capitalize Network Effects for Influence:** Leverage interconnected systems to amplify impact.

46. **Be Predictable in Cooperative Settings:** Foster trust by acting consistently and reliably.

47. **Compromise Strategically, Not Emotionally:** Negotiate with logic, not sentiment.

48. **Maximize Joint Gains in Team-Ups:** Align efforts to achieve shared success.

49. **Establish Harmony Between Transparency and Secrecy:** Balance openness with discretion for optimal collaboration.

50. **Foster a Reputation for Fair Actions:** Build trust by consistently demonstrating fairness.

51. **Turn Enemies into Allies:** Transform adversaries into partners through shared goals.

52. **Concentrate on the Shared Objective:** Keep partnerships focused on common interests.

53. **Generate Value Before Asking for Value:** Prove your worth before seeking reciprocity.

54. **Be Generous Without Being Exploitable:** Offer support while protecting your interests.

55. **Align Incentives to Sustain Cooperation:** Ensure everyone benefits equally to maintain partnerships.

56. **Honor Loyalty Proactively:** Reward steadfastness to strengthen relationships.

57. **Forge Coalitions Around Shared Interests:** Unite groups with common objectives for greater impact.
58. **Avoid Overpromising in Groups:** Manage expectations to maintain credibility.
59. **Communicate Clearly to Reduce Misunderstandings:** Use transparency to prevent conflict.
60. **Exit Teams Gracefully When Necessary:** End partnerships positively to preserve goodwill.

Part 4: Adaptive Strategies

61. **Anticipate Game-Changing Trends:** Stay ahead by identifying transformative shifts early.
62. **Be the First to Spot Weak Signals:** Detect subtle changes that signal future developments.
63. **Apply Change as a Well-Designed Asset:** Leverage change to your advantage through planning.
64. **Develop Options for Uncertain Futures:** Prepare flexible strategies for multiple scenarios.
65. **Use Real Options to Hedge Strategies:** Invest in opportunities while minimizing risks.
66. **Develop Contingency Plans for Key Obstacles:** Prepare for challenges before they arise.
67. **Test Assumptions Before Acting:** Validate your plans by questioning their foundations.
68. **Try Experimentation for Growth:** Innovate by testing and iterating ideas.
69. **Turn Failures into Stepping Stones for Progress:** Learn from setbacks to move forward stronger.
70. **Adapt Plans in Real Time:** Stay flexible to react effectively as situations evolve.
71. **Detect Hidden Patterns in Chaos:** Find order in complexity to guide decisions.
72. **Use Contrarian Thinking to Your Advantage:** Embrace unconventional ideas to uncover opportunities.
73. **Stay Agile in Dynamic Environments:** Move quickly and flexibly to stay ahead of change.

74. **Exploit Adversaries' Rigidity:** Use others' resistance to adapt as a weakness.

75. **Be Unpredictable to Stay Ahead:** Keep competitors guessing by avoiding predictable patterns.

76. **Diversify Your Cheat Sheet:** Build a broad toolkit to adapt to any scenario.

77. **Counterpoise Risk and Reward Over Time:** Balance short-term risk with long-term rewards.

78. **Thrive in Nonlinear Scenarios:** Embrace complexity to find opportunities in chaos.

79. **Prepare for Worst-Case Scenarios:** Anticipate challenges and plan accordingly.

80. **Apply the OODA Loop: Observe, Orient, Decide, Act:** Use this iterative framework to adapt quickly.

Part 5: Advanced Strategies

81. **Orchestrate Complex Systems for Advantage:** Align diverse elements to create synergy.

82. **Manage Trade-Offs with Precision:** Balance conflicting priorities for optimal results.

83. **Engineer Irreversible Advantages:** Build strengths that competitors cannot replicate.

84. **Use Authority to Multiply Impact:** Leverage influence to inspire and lead effectively.

85. **Turn Opponents' Strengths Into Vulnerabilities:** Exploit competitors' overreliance on their strengths.

86. **Harness the Wisdom of the Crowd:** Use collective intelligence for better decisions.

87. **Command the Precision of Timing:** Act at the perfect moment for maximum impact.

88. **Uncover Unique Perspectives to Lead with an Edge:** See what others miss to innovate effectively.

89. **Be Relentless in Follow-Through:** Ensure consistent execution to achieve goals.

90. **Apply the Prisoner's Dilemma to Real Life:** Balance cooperation and competition strategically.

91. **Engineer Scarcity to Drive Value:** Use limited availability to increase demand.

92. **Use Game-Theoretic Modeling to Predict Next Steps:** Anticipate others' actions to plan effectively.

93. **Identify and Gain From Bottlenecks in Systems:** Optimize constraints to unlock potential.

94. **Redefine the Rules of the Game:** Change the framework of competition to your advantage.

95. **Turn Opposing Forces Into Complementors:** Align with competitors to create mutual benefits.

96. **Always Leave Room for Reversal:** Build flexibility into plans to adapt to change.

97. **Stockpile Reserves for Important Moments:** Prepare resources for critical opportunities.

98. **Design Self-Reinforcing Systems:** Create feedback loops that drive long-term success.

99. **End Games with Grace and Foresight:** Conclude strategically to preserve relationships and reputation.

100. **Achieve Strategic Mastery Through Continuous Education:** Commit to lifelong learning to refine your expertise.

Appendix B: Section and Chapter Outline

This appendix provides a straightforward outline of all the chapters in the book, organized by section. Use this as a quick guide to locate chapters or revisit specific topics as needed.

Part 1: Foundational Strategies (Chapters 1–20)

- Play the Long Game, Not the Next Move
- Begin with the End in Mind
- Prioritize Clarity Over Speed
- Leverage Asymmetry in Resources
- Embrace Iterative Progress
- Balance Offensive and Defensive Moves
- Understand the Zero-Sum Game
- Find Win-Win Opportunities
- Evaluate Trade-Offs in Every Decision
- Don't Confuse Luck with Strategy
- Cultivate Tactical Patience
- Harness the Power of Perception
- Simplify Complex Options
- Always Ask "Why?" Twice
- Avoid Overcommitting Help
- Be the First Mover When It Counts
- Follow the Nash Equilibrium

- Be Predictable in Cooperative Settings
- Compromise Strategically, Not Emotionally
- Maximize Joint Gains in Team-Ups
- Establish Harmony Between Transparency and Secrecy
- Foster a Reputation for Fair Actions
- Turn Enemies into Allies
- Concentrate on the Shared Objective
- Generate Value Before Asking for Value
- Be Generous Without Being Exploitable
- Align Incentives to Sustain Cooperation
- Honor Loyalty Proactively
- Forge Coalitions Around Shared Interests
- Avoid Overpromising in Groups
- Communicate Clearly to Reduce Misunderstandings
- Exit Teams Gracefully When Necessary

Part 4: Adaptive Strategies (Chapters 61–80)

- Anticipate Game-Changing Trends
- Be the First to Spot Weak Signals
- Apply Change as a Well-Designed Asset
- Develop Options for Uncertain Futures
- Use Real Options to Hedge Strategies
- Develop Contingency Plans for Key Obstacles
- Test Assumptions Before Acting
- Try Experimentation for Growth
- Turn Failures into Stepping Stones for Progress
- Adapt Plans in Real Time
- Detect Hidden Patterns in Chaos
- Use Contrarian Thinking to Your Advantage
- Stay Agile in Dynamic Environments
- Exploit Adversaries' Rigidity
- Be Unpredictable to Stay Ahead
- Diversify Your Cheat Sheet

- Counterpoise Risk and Reward Over Time
- Thrive in Nonlinear Scenarios
- Prepare for Worst-Case Scenarios
- Apply the OODA Loop: Observe, Orient, Decide, Act

Part 5: Advanced Strategies (Chapters 81–100)

- Orchestrate Complex Systems for Advantage
- Manage Trade-Offs with Precision
- Engineer Irreversible Advantages
- Use Authority to Multiply Impact
- Turn Opponents' Strengths Into Vulnerabilities
- Harness the Wisdom of the Crowd
- Command the Precision of Timing
- Uncover Unique Perspectives to Lead with an Edge
- Be Relentless in Follow-Through
- Apply the Prisoner's Dilemma to Real Life
- Engineer Scarcity to Drive Value
- Use Game-Theoretic Modeling to Predict Next Steps
- Identify and Gain From Bottlenecks in Systems
- Redefine the Rules of the Game
- Turn Opposing Forces Into Complementors
- Always Leave Room for Reversal
- Stockpile Reserves for Important Moments
- Design Self-Reinforcing Systems
- End Games with Grace and Foresight
- Achieve Strategic Mastery Through Continuous Education

Appendix C: Practice Scenarios

This appendix provides 15 real-world practice scenarios to help you apply the strategies outlined in this book. Each scenario presents a problem statement followed by a challenge that asks you to identify which strategy (or strategies) from the chapters can be used to address the situation. Use this section to sharpen your strategic thinking and strengthen your ability to adapt these principles to various situations.

Scenario 1: Reviving a Declining Product Line

Problem Statement: Your company's once-popular product is now losing market share to competitors offering newer, more innovative solutions. Internal stakeholders are divided on whether to continue investing in the product or phase it out.

Challenge: Apply strategies such as **"Turn Failures into Stepping Stones for Progress" (Chapter 69)** or **"Redefine the Rules of the Game" (Chapter 94)** to identify how to reposition or transform the product to regain relevance.

Scenario 2: Navigating a High-Stakes Negotiation

Problem Statement: You're negotiating a critical partnership with a larger company that has greater leverage. They've proposed terms that seem one-sided but essential for moving forward.

Challenge: Use strategies like **"Capture High Ground in Negotiations" (Chapter 27)** and **"Compromise Strategically, Not Emotionally" (Chapter 47)** to secure favorable terms while maintaining the partnership.

Scenario 3: Managing a Team in Conflict

Problem Statement: Two key team members have conflicting priorities and their disagreements are affecting the overall performance of the team. The organization cannot afford to lose either individual.

Challenge: Apply **"Lay the Foundation for Trust Before You Request Collaboration" (Chapter 41)** and **"Concentrate on the Shared Objective" (Chapter 52)** to realign the team's focus and resolve tensions.

Scenario 4: Launching a New Product in a Saturated Market

Problem Statement: Your company plans to launch a product in a market dominated by established players. Resources are limited, and you need to make an impact quickly.

Challenge: Use **"Be the First Mover When It Counts" (Chapter 16)** or **"Exploit Adversaries' Rigidity" (Chapter 74)** to identify a niche or unique approach that can differentiate your product.

Scenario 5: Addressing Customer Dissatisfaction

Problem Statement: A key customer segment has expressed dissatisfaction with your service, leading to declining sales and potential reputational damage.

Challenge: Apply **"Harness the Power of Perception" (Chapter 12)** and **"Generate Value Before Asking for Value" (Chapter 53)** to rebuild trust and loyalty with your customers.

Scenario 6: Facing Aggressive Competition

Problem Statement: A rival company has launched a price war, aggressively undercutting your offerings to capture market share. Your margins are too tight to match their pricing.

Challenge: Use **"Force Your Competitors to Overextend" (Chapter 39)** or **"Neutralize Emerging Risks Before They Escalate" (Chapter 35)** to develop a non-price-based strategy to counteract the competition.

Scenario 7: Managing Limited Resources

Problem Statement: Your department has been tasked with delivering an ambitious project but has only half the resources originally allocated. Deadlines are tight, and expectations remain high.

Challenge: Leverage **"Leverage Asymmetry in Resources" (Chapter 4)** and **"Build Redundancies for Resilience" (Chapter 18)** to optimize resource use and deliver results efficiently.

Scenario 8: Responding to Industry Disruption

Problem Statement: A technological breakthrough is reshaping your industry, leaving traditional players at risk of obsolescence. Your organization has been slow to adapt.

Challenge: Apply **"Anticipate Game-Changing Trends" (Chapter 61)** and **"Adapt Plans in Real Time" (Chapter 70)** to create a strategy that embraces innovation and positions your organization for success.

Scenario 9: Strengthening a Weak Partnership

Problem Statement: A strategic partnership with another company is underperforming, and trust between both parties has eroded. The partnership is still critical to achieving long-term goals.

Challenge: Use **"Align Incentives to Sustain Cooperation" (Chapter 55)** and **"Be Generous Without Being Exploitable" (Chapter 54)** to rebuild trust and improve collaboration.

Scenario 10: Preparing for a Worst-Case Scenario

Problem Statement: A potential economic downturn threatens your company's operations. Leadership is divided on how much to invest in contingency planning versus staying focused on current projects.

Challenge: Leverage **"Prepare for Worst-Case Scenarios" (Chapter 79)** and **"Stockpile Reserves for Important Moments" (Chapter 97)** to ensure readiness without compromising current objectives.

Scenario 11: Encouraging Innovation in a Stagnant Team

Problem Statement: Your team is hesitant to take risks or experiment, leading to a lack of fresh ideas and slow progress.

Challenge: Apply **"Try Experimentation for Growth" (Chapter 68)** and **"Use Contrarian Thinking to Your Advantage" (Chapter 72)** to foster a culture of creativity and calculated risk-taking.

Scenario 12: Turning a Competitor into a Collaborator

Problem Statement: A rival company has been targeting your market aggressively, but there's potential for collaboration to expand opportunities for both sides.

Challenge: Use **"Turn Opposing Forces Into Complementors" (Chapter 95)** and **"Forge Coalitions Around Shared Interests" (Chapter 57)** to establish common ground and create a win-win partnership.

Scenario 13: Shifting Internal Perceptions

Problem Statement: Your department is perceived as a support function rather than a driver of value, limiting your influence within the organization.

Challenge: Leverage **"Harness the Power of Perception" (Chapter 12)** and **"Be the First to Spot Weak Signals" (Chapter 62)** to redefine your role and demonstrate strategic value.

Scenario 14: Competing Against a First Mover

Problem Statement: A competitor has launched a new product that's gaining momentum. You're tasked with finding a way to counteract their lead without mimicking their strategy.

Challenge: Use **"Exploit Adversaries' Rigidity" (Chapter 74)** and **"Command the Precision of Timing" (Chapter 87)** to find innovative ways to regain market attention.

Scenario 15: Exiting a Market with Grace

Problem Statement: Your company needs to exit an underperforming market, but doing so risks alienating existing customers and damaging your brand reputation.

Challenge: Apply **"End Games with Grace and Foresight" (Chapter 99)** and **"Always Leave Room for Reversal" (Chapter 96)** to ensure a smooth transition that minimizes negative impacts.

Appendix D: Strategic Application Checklist

This checklist is designed to help you integrate the strategies from this book into your daily life, decision-making, and long-term planning. Use it as a guide to ensure that you consistently apply the principles and practices outlined in this book. Each point highlights a key area of focus with actionable steps to reinforce strategic thinking and execution.

1. Define Your Long-Term Vision

- Write down where you want to be in 5, 10, or 20 years.
- Break your vision into measurable goals.
- Regularly revisit and adjust your vision as needed.

2. Prioritize Actions for Maximum Impact

- Identify the tasks that will make the biggest difference.
- Use the 80/20 rule to focus on high-impact efforts.
- Set deadlines to create urgency for important actions.

3. Balance Risk and Reward in Decisions

- Assess both short-term and long-term consequences.
- Identify worst-case scenarios and prepare for them.
- Take calculated risks when the potential reward is worth it.

4. Build Relationships Strategically

- Network with people who align with your goals.
- Offer value before asking for favors or collaboration.
- Foster trust through consistent and reliable actions.

5. Stay Flexible and Ready to Pivot

- Regularly review your progress and identify areas for change.
- Develop contingency plans for key goals.
- Embrace failure as an opportunity to adapt and improve.

6. Use Perception to Your Advantage

- Present yourself and your work in ways that align with your goals.
- Pay attention to how others view your actions and adjust as needed.
- Communicate clearly and confidently to shape perceptions.

7. Simplify Complex Decisions

- Break down big decisions into smaller, manageable parts.
- Focus on what's essential and eliminate distractions.
- Use decision-making frameworks to clarify your options.

8. Invest in Lifelong Learning

- Dedicate time to reading, courses, or mentorship.
- Stay updated on trends and shifts in your field or industry.
- Reflect on past successes and failures to extract lessons.

9. Act with Patience and Precision

- Avoid rushing into decisions without sufficient information.
- Wait for the right moment to take action.
- Stay disciplined and focused, even when progress feels slow.

10. Cultivate Win-Win Outcomes

- Look for ways to create mutual benefit in negotiations or collaborations.

- Approach conflicts with the goal of finding shared ground.
- Build solutions that address the needs of all parties involved.

11. Plan for the Unexpected

- Identify potential risks and plan responses in advance.
- Build redundancies into your work or processes to handle surprises.
- Test your plans with small-scale experiments to uncover blind spots.

12. Leverage Strengths—Yours and Others'

- Identify your unique skills and focus on them.
- Delegate tasks that align with others' strengths.
- Collaborate with people whose skills complement your own.

13. Stay Ahead by Spotting Trends Early

- Monitor industry developments and weak signals of change.
- Regularly discuss trends with peers or mentors to gain diverse insights.
- Adjust your strategies to align with emerging opportunities.

14. Keep Relationships Strong

- Check in regularly with key contacts, even when there's no immediate need.
- Show appreciation for others' contributions.
- Actively listen and respond thoughtfully to build rapport.

15. Execute Relentlessly

- Break projects into actionable steps and tackle them daily.
- Track progress and hold yourself accountable.
- Celebrate small wins to maintain momentum and motivation.

Pro Tip: Make Strategy a Habit

The key to mastering strategy is consistency. Integrate strategic thinking into your daily routines by using this checklist regularly. Reflect on your actions, evaluate outcomes, and adjust your approach as needed. Small, deliberate steps taken every day will compound over time, transforming your mindset and ensuring long-term success. Remember, strategy isn't a one-time exercise — it's a way of life.

Here's another book by Quinn Voss that you might like

www.ingramcontent.com/pod-product-compliance
Lightning Source LLC
Chambersburg PA
CBHW061554120626

46550CB00004B/1485